D1552959

BELLED BUZZARDS, HUCKSTERS AND GRIEVING SPECTERS

Appalachian Tales: Strange, True & Legendary

Gary Carden
Nina Anderson

DOWN HOME

Down Home Press, Asheboro, N.C.

NEW HANOVER COUNTY
PUBLIC LIBRARY
201 CHESTNUT STREET
WILMINGTON N.C. 28401

Copyright 1994 by Nina Anderson, Gary Carden

All rights reserved. No part of this book may be reproduced by any means without permission of the publisher, except for brief passages in reviews and articles.

ISBN 1-878086-28-6

Library of Congress Number 94-070669

Printed in the United States of America

Cover Design by Ginger Flynt Harris

Book Design by Ginger Flynt Harris

2 3 4 5 6 7 8 9 10

Down Home Press
PO Box 4126
Asheboro, N.C. 27204

Acknowledgments

Nina L. Anderson

To every person who has ever told me a wonderful story, to the North Carolina Arts Council and to the scores of folks willing to talk to me I owe a special thank you. Dr. James Dooley and Furman Raby were of special help by pointing me in directions I wouldn't have considered. More than once I was reminded that for all the dire predictions of what technology has done to our lives, we humans still relish a fascinating tale.

Gary Carden

I owe thanks to:

The Friends of Hunter Library at Western Carolina University who provided me with a membership and gave me access to their research material;

Richard Wilson of Sylva who remembers "Sidney Lanier Day" at the Sylva Elementary School. (He is also a direct descendant of Dick Wilson, the murder victim in "The Hanging of Jack Lambert");

Manley Wade Wellman who has told some of these stories before;

C. R. Sumner;

George Frizzell in the Archives Section of Hunter Library;

The spirit of Dr. Robert Lee Madison whose influence is evident throughout this book;

Marilyn McMinn McCredie who had rather talk than write;

Collin and Scott;

and above all, Dot Jackson.

Contents

PART I

GHOSTS, BELLED BUZZARDS, GRIEVING SPECTERS AND DEATH'S PALE MESSENGER

INTRODUCTION

Ghost: the outward and visible sign of
an inward fear.
— Ambrose Bierce

There is something that loves the night. It battens on moonbeams and lives in moist, shadowy places. While we sleep, its eyes are open, and as we lie helpless in our beds, it races from shadow to shadow, exulting in its power. The night belongs to it as surely as we are creatures of the sun. (Well, most of us, anyway.) In our ignorance we try to classify the creatures of the night. Vampires, we say, live in Hungary, and banshees live in Ireland. The Nunnehi live beneath the earth in southern Appalachia, and Hecate haunts Grecian crossroads in the dark of the moon. To everything, its place and season.

Consider this. Perhaps it is all the same. Perhaps the something that loves the night is everywhere, and it is neither "good" or "evil," lacking definition or character. It is waiting patiently to be born. It is waiting for us to give it a name.

Before the white man came, the Cherokees told stories of the creatures that shunned the harsh light of day, and they were as varied as their sun-loving counterparts. The Yunwi Tsunsdi, "Little People," are mischievous, but they frequently bring lost children home, stopping in the shadows at the edge of the woods while the children run towards the village calling their mother's

3

name. The invisible Nunnehi watch the Cherokees with compassionate eyes, sometimes warning them of approaching danger. The deadly Uktena, the horned snake with the flashing crystal in its head, waits patiently in the dark river gorges for a lone hunter and Raven Mocker comes in the night to the sick child's bed ... comes to consume the child's liver. The shadow-dwelling creatures had hundreds of names and functions, each a facet of the ancient force that is always there.

When the white man drove the Cherokees from the Southern Highlands, the creatures fled, too. The Nunnehi went deeper beneath the earth, the Yunwi Tsunsdi climbed higher, fleeing the white man's roads, axes and guns. Finally, their frail voices faded. So, too, vanished the Uktena and Raven Mocker. But the something that loves moonlight and shadow merely waited. In time, the white man would give it new names, new parts to play.

So, the settlers lived, rejoiced, suffered and died. They committed acts of unimaginable cruelty, suffered from unrequitted love, performed noble and selfless deeds and sometimes died in abject misery. The Grieving Mother of Mount Hebron. The Belled Buzzard. The White Horse That Comes at Twilight. And so, its time come 'round again, the patient "something" rose among the insubstantial night shadows to don new costumes and assume new roles.

G.C.

THE GRIEVING MOTHER OF MOUNT HEBRON

She never speaks, but her gestures and the pain etched in her pale face are eloquent. She stands on the side of the Mount Hebron Church Road in Henderson County dressed totally in black: poke bonnet, shawl and longskirt. Those who have seen her standing in her patch of moonlight beside a huge poplar invariably comment on the intensity of her misery.

"She's not what you would normally think of as a spook," said one of the drovers who had seen her on numerous occasions. "She won't frighten you, but she might make you cry."

She seems to be in the grip of despair. Twisting her hands together, she stares down the road, her eyes searching — searching.

I think she wants help," said a young man who frequently traveled the Mount Hebron Road at the turn of the century. "I'm accustomed to seeing her there, and if you approach her, she will give you a heartrending, beseeching look. It's like a desperate plea for help."

Many have attempted to talk to her.

"What's wrong, ma'm? Can you tell me what is wrong?"

Her gestures become frantic; she seems both terror-stricken and beseeching. Invariably, she begins to retreat, and finally, she turns and darts behind the great tree. Those who rush after her, expecting to find the pitiful figure crouched behind the trunk, find nothing. She is gone.

There is a story about two farm boys who once rushed her, one to the left and the other to the right. Racing behind the tree, they simply collided with each other. Nothing was there but dark woods, moonlight and insubstantial shadows.

There is a story, though. If it did not exist in fact, someone would have invented it in fancy. It is the story of a widow who came with her young son in 1805 or thereabouts to the dark forests of what would become Mount Hebron. The son found a gigantic tree which was hollow, and being a clever lad, converted it into a temporary home. Later, he built a cabin, but settlers in the region remember the tree with mitered windows and a door. Then the son befriended another young man whose family had moved to the region, and his friend told him of an impending war.

"We should go to war, you and I! It would be a great adventure, and besides it is our duty to do so."

And so they did. The widow was heartbroken. Despite her pleas, the son was obstinate. Duty called, he said, and besides, "We won't be gone long." When the two young men did not return, the widow and the mother of the other young man set out to find their wayward children and bring them home. The story says that the two women walked to Virginia. Eventually, the other young man's mother returned.

"My son is dead," she told her husband. "He is buried in Virginia."

But the widow did not return for many years. Even then, her neighbors said she refused to give up hope. Because she had not found his grave, she was confident that her son was still alive. He would be home any day now. Each evening, she went to the Mount Hebron Road, a tireless sentinel. When young men came up the road driving horses, cattle or pigs, the widow would peer beseechingly into their faces. Is this him? And then, seeing a stranger's face, she would weep inconsolably. Turning, she would dart behind the great poplar.

The Southern Highlands are filled with the ghosts of grieving women. They stand on the banks of rivers and lakes staring into the murdering water. They haunt suicide bridges, mountain trails and abandoned mines. Sometimes they are seen in graveyards, where they kneel before tombstones, their intangible fingers tracing the names in the stone. Like a Mobius strip, they seem doomed to eternal repetition. In Mitchell County, a young woman dressed in 18th century garb descends a staircase and rushes to a verandah where she peers expectantly into the darkness and then vanishes. The old house has been abandoned for over one-hundred years, but on moonlight nights in the fall of the year "something" lives there. The "Woman in White" at the Old Calvary Episcopal Church in Fletcher, N.C. merely drifts through the moonlit cemetery, pauses briefly by a row of ancient, eroded stones and vanishes. A rendezvous perhaps? Is this a visible memory of a night when someone failed to keep an appointment? Perhaps, one night, he will be there.

G.C.

THE BELLED BUZZARD

In earlier times, the people of the Southern Highlands tended to regard death as a highly significant event. Nineteenth century eulogies were heartfelt, sentimental and lengthy. Newspapers devoted columns to comments from friends of the deceased, death-bed statements and poetic fanfares. But the marvels of communication — radio, movies and the daily paper quickly brought an awareness of how prosaic death really is. The passing of a retired minister, an event once announced by tolling bells, funeral pageantry, memorial services and black-bordered eulogies has become a commonplace event. Our "notable deceased" is reduced to a single millet seed dropped into the ponderous mills of death. Each hour, thousands are sped on their way.

But there was a time when the final leave-taking of the "great and near-great" was surrounded with portents and omens. Take the story of the Belled Buzzard, for example.

Early historians call him "the winged harbinger of death." He usually came at twilight, his great funereal wings slowly rising and falling as he crossed farm lands and forests. And, of course, the bell was tolling ... the bell that hung from the messenger's neck. Dong...Dong....

9

The reverberations of each note fade to silence before the next note is born. Families would rush into the yard to watch the buzzard fly unerringly to its destination — the home of a retired statesman, general or plantation owner. Sorrowing relatives gathered around the death bed would hear it approaching. Dong...Dong. And the dying heard it, too. Stories relate how stricken patriarchs raised their heads, saying, "Listen! He has come."

The buzzard did not come for everyone. There are no stories about the aerial bell tolling for children, mothers dying of childbed fever or farmers struck down by accident or disease. The ominous bird comes only for those who aspired to greatness and achieved it...men of power and wealth. Robert Henry heard it in the mountain fastness of Clay County. (See "Iona's Son") According to an old family story Henry heard the mournful knell three times: once for each of his two capable and brilliant sons and once for himself.

During the first quarter of this century, there were numerous sightings in North Carolina, Tennessee and Georgia. On March 8, 1924, two Georgia hunters were startled by the tolling bell, and they turned to see the buzzard which was flying very close to the ground. Georgia newspapers carried articles with such captions as, "Belled Buzzard Back in Worth County."

The last recorded sighting of death's messenger was on a Friday evening in Leicester, N. C., August 13, 1926. The witness, a farmer named Ed Rhymer was quoted as saying, "At first, I thought my cows was in the corn again." Rhymer went out to take a look and saw the great bird flying slowly up the valley. Rhymer listened to the fading dirge of the bell and wondered about its destination. Apparently Rhymer was not the least apprehensive about his own fate. Several days later, another man, Eugene Sluder, in nearby Newfound said he saw the bird flying point in a formation of four. The buzzards "were heading west," he said, but only the leader was belled.

Migrating? Why not? Electrical power lines had spread up the Pigeon and the French Broad, and in many places the night had been turned today. What distant sanctuary could give safe harbor to an old-fashioned bird who believed in death's amenities? A place where the final leave-taking was still observed with pomp, solemnity and ceremony?

Several years ago, a young man in an isolated rural area of Arkansas captured a buzzard. Remembering stories that his grandmother had told him about the doleful tolling of the belled buzzard, the young man tied a bell around the old bird's neck and released it. During the next week, inhabitants of several counties reported sightings.

"He is back!" they said. The buzzard roosted on barns and circled the local nursing home. Dong...Dong. A retired politician called law enforcement officers.

"He is in a stand of locust behind my house," he said. "I know we don't believe in such stuff anymore, but he is making me nervous."

Now, that is gratifying.

G.C.

Note: In the lowlands of Appalachia, where the rugged mountains begin to give way to rolling pasture and wealthy farmers, there were no reports of belled buzzards. After all, these were people of substance and status. Any portents of approaching doom should be more dignified. Let the rude scavenger keep to the mountain heights; here the coming of death was announced by a white horse.

THE WHITE HORSE THAT COMES AT TWILIGHT

The stories about death's pale horse are numerous in Appalachia, but there are certain stock ingredients: a stricken patriarch, a son dispatched to a nearby town for a physician or medicine, and last, but not least, a tree-lined drive. As night's shadows fall, the sick man's family gathers on the verandah to watch for the return of the son. And then, they hear it — the sound of a racing horse. Peering down the dark drive, they see it — a white horse racing up the drive. Someone observes, "I thought John was riding the roan."

And someone replies, "He was."

But this is not a roan, and the rider is not John. The hoof beats thunder on until the rider (cloaked, of course) swerves in a sweeping arc around the house. Abruptly, there is silence. No diminishing hoof-beats, just sudden silence. From within the house comes the cry of the dying patriarch. "I heard it! It was the white horse, wasn't it?" The belated return of the son finds the family gathered around the death bed. Too late, too late; death has come and gone.

The pale horse has gone the way of the belled buzzard. Perhaps he grazes in a western meadow where it is always twilight, surrounded by other archaic phantoms — white deer, speaking owls and candle-bearing specters. They cannot live in a world filled with neon, sodium arcs and interstate highways. A white horse and a cloaked rider on I-40 would merely become an eccentric traffic hazard. What has replaced him? What would be the modern equivalent of death's messenger? An insubstantial ambulance? Spectral paramedics? Perhaps a silver hearse that purrs up the drive and then vanishes. Is it waiting out there beyond the reach of street lights, waiting for you to say its name?

G.C.

THE PHANTOM MILLERS

About fifteen years after the Civil War, William G. Ziegler and Ben Grosscup began collecting material for their book, *The Heart of the Alleghenies*. Their travels brought them to Graham County, North Carolina. One summer afternoon, while walking an old wagon trail with a man Zeigler identifies as "Mr. Staley, an intelligent, elderly farmer," the two found themselves near an abandoned mill.

Zeigler's curiosity prompted a number of questions about the origin of the mill and its dilapidated condition. Staley said he had built the mill to avoid traveling the eighteen miles to Murphy for flour and meal. Sensing that the farmer seemed reluctant to discuss the reason for abandoning his mill, Zeigler knew he was on to a story. After several more questions, Zeigler's persistence paid off.

Surrounded by the sounds of the turbulent mill stream, the two men seated themselves in the back of the mill with their feet dangling above the old wheel, now green and rotten. Zeigler noted that the spray and mist drifting upwards from the boiling waters gave him an occasional chill, but in a few moments he would forget his discomfort as Staley talked.

Staley said he had moved to Graham County in the 1840's and had immediately selected the mill site. Within a few months, the mill not only provided flour for his family but grew into a modest livelihood. Staley's mill became popular with the farmers of the region, but then a number of unpleasant events occurred.

15

Staley arrived one morning to find the wheel had stopped. While investigating, he was horrified to find the body of a young man trapped in the broken paddle. Although the dead man was quickly identified, the manner of his death remained a mystery. Not long afterwards, a neighbor's child fell to its death through a trap door in the mill. Then the rumors started.

Staley learned that many of his neighbors felt there was a spell on the mill. Travelers in the area developed a new trail to avoid it. Even the local ne'er-do-wells who frequently slipped into the building at night to grind corn without paying for the privilege stopped coming. Staley was distressed to hear stories about his "hainted mill," and within a short time, the operation was reduced to only meeting the needs of Staley's family. But a greater tragedy was yet to come.

On a spring day in 1861, Staley and his younger brother arrived at the mill to do some minor repairs. Leaving his brother in the building, Staley ventured into the woods for "a second-growth hickory" which he needed for a support timber. Suddenly, rising above the ever-present din of the turbulent creek, Staley heard angry voices. Then there was a shot.

Racing back down the hill, Staley noted that he did not see anyone running away, and since most of the timber surrounding the mill had been cleared, there was little opportunity for concealment. Hurrying to the mill, Staley's worst fear was realized. His brother lay dying on the floor.

As life ebbed from the young man's body, Staley sensed that the murderer was still present. Convinced that the culprit could not have escaped without being seen, Staley searched the mill. Finding nothing, he ventured outside to find that the sky had darkened and the wind was rising. A major storm was brewing. With the first flash of lightning, Staley took shelter inside the mill. As he turned to observe the storm from the doorway, a gigantic ash, not thirty feet from the mill entrance, was sundered from top to bole.

His sight gradually returned, but with it came strange sounds. Beneath the beat of the rain and the wind, which caused the mill to rattle and creak, Staley heard a human voice, a muffled sound that alternated between weeping and moaning. At times it ceased, but then would come a sharp, agonized cry followed by more weeping. Staley attempted to rationalize the sounds as nothing more than wind and water, but the cries continued throughout the night, stopping only when the first dim rays of daylight seeped through the walls.

Two farm hands, sent by Staley's worried wife, arrived the following morning. The job of removing the young brother's body was made doubly difficult by the presence of the great ash at the base of a hollow oak near the mill's door. The tree partially blocked the entrance.

Several days after his brother's funeral, Staley went to Murphy on business only to learn he had been drafted into the Confederate Army. His leave-taking was abrupt, and for the next four years his only knowledge of his abandoned mill came from his wife's letters. She told him that the stories about the "hainted mill" had increased. In fact, during the week following young Staley's death, several travelers told of hearing moans and cries from it. Shortly afterwards, people reported strange lights, eerie cries, and shadowy figures moving inside the mill. Many of the neighbors also believed that bread baked from the "hainted mill" was stained with blood. Staley learned that people of the area avoided it, even in daylight.

When he returned home after the war, Staley was told that although his family had employed a mill operator, the employee had abandoned the job after only a few days. Realizing that his neighbors were taking their corn to a mill that was both expensive and distant, Staley decided to renovate the operation, and he asked several neighbors to help him.

The friends repeated stories about ghostly figures flitting along the mill race on moonless nights. To test the truth of such tales, Staley asked some neighbors to accompany him to the site. There they discovered that the grinding stones were clean and coated with fresh flour. Staley felt sure someone was using the mill at night. One of his neighbors agreed but added that he doubted the visitors were flesh and blood.

When Staley suggested a nighttime visit to the mill, only one stout-hearted neighbor agreed to accompany him. Hiding in a thicket some fifty feet below the raceway, the two men waited for hours until a series of owl

17

hoots came. Shortly afterwards, the calls came again, but nearer. Then a light flared in the mill, and a number of ghostly figures that seemed to glow began pouring corn into the hopper.

Moving closer, Staley and his companion heard, above the sound of stone grinding on stone, the soft whisper of speech — not English but Cherokee!

Convinced he had solved the mystery, Staley fired his rifle into the mill. Instantly the light extinguished, followed by the sounds of several bodies crashing through the thicket on the far side of the mill.

The following morning, Staley discovered an abandoned bag of corn, some ground meal and a few drops of blood in the grinding room. The mystery was solved. The Cherokees, who knew of the superstitions surrounding the white man's mill, decided to use the rumors to their advantage. Each time they arrived at the mill, the Cherokees coated themselves with flour. If anyone approached the mill, the Cherokees wafted about, making ghostly cries.

Having convinced his neighbors that his mill was not "spelled," Staley set to work repairing the structure. During the renovation, he and several helpers began removing the fallen ash that had lain in front of the mill for more than four years. As they were moving a large section of the trunk which lay against the hollow oak, the men made a grisly discovery.

A pair of boots stood inside the hollow tree. When the boots were taken out, a full skeleton clattered out, too. Personal belongings in the tattered clothing identified the remains as those of a neighbor who had disappeared four years ago. Everyone thought he had died in the war. Among the rotting clothing and personal effects was a revolver — the one that had killed Staley's younger brother.

And so the final mystery was solved. Except for one item. No one ever knew the motive for the murder.

If we reconstruct the details of this "ghostly" mystery, we find a terrible detail. On that fatal day, the murderer, seeing no means of escaping undetected, hid himself in the hollow oak. When the lightning-riven ash fell against his sanctuary, the trapped man was probably injured, but alive. The plaintive wails and cries Staley heard throughout that stormy night are explained.

But what about the cries heard for several days and nights *after* the storm? Cries that sounded like faint pleas for help. How long did young Staley's murderer live?

And as for the final abandonment of the mill, Staley told his visitor it had nothing to do with "spells" or "haints." He contemplated the awful fate of his brother's murderer and found that the painful memories evoked by the fallen tree made it impossible for him to operate the mill. Staley halted the renovation.

Soon afterwards, a flash flood carried away the mill race. Gradually nature began the process of removing the mill by eroding the timbers, a process that, to Staley, resembled the healing of a wound, or the fading of a scar.

G.C.

THE LINEBACK GHOST

He had grown up knowing about the Lineback ghost. It might have been the first story Philo Pritchard heard as a child. It was certainly the one he thought about the most.

No one in the North Carolina mountain community of Avery County doubted the existence of the ghost. The booger was obviously part of Mr. Lineback's store, and the reason for the haint's existence went back many years.

A family of Irish peddlers, husband, wife and daughter had come through the community selling fine linens. They had done well and been paid in gold, so they were leaving on horseback when they were apparently attacked and murdered. No one knew for certain what happened, because only the bodies were found. The bags of gold were gone, but everyone agreed it seemed fairly obvious that the family had been killed for their money.

When Mr. Lineback decided to build a store near the place of the triple murder, a ghost appeared to help. The ghost hammered nails and put up boards during the evenings, and often the ghost worked as fast as two or three men. With so much free assistance, Lineback's store was completed and ready for business long before anyone expected.

A lean-to shed was added to the back of the store and a cot placed inside so someone could sleep at the store and protect the business since the Lineback family did not live in the building.

At first, Mr. Lineback tried to work in the store at night, but the ghost was a nuisance. While Mr. Lineback tried to stock the shelves, the ghost would blow out the candle. When he relit the candle, a puff of air that came from nowhere would send the room into darkness again. The merchant tried to continue working by keeping the lighted candle close to his body, but the ghost jumped on his back and extinguished the flame.

When other people were hired to sleep in the lean-to and watch the store, the ghost made so much noise they couldn't sleep. Several told of hearing the ghost dropping one-hundred pound bags of unground coffee and "shackling and shuffling along" as the ghost went "a-clerkin' and a-tradin', a-waitin' on customers and wrappin' up bundles." The ghost even measured cloth, cut it, wrapped it up and recorded the sale in the store ledger.

When heavy sleepers tried guard duty, the ghost found other ways to rout the visitor. In the midst of a solid sleep, the bed covers would be pulled off and the ghost would lean over the cot to display big, blood-red eyes and teeth shaped like pumpkin seeds. None of the guards awakened so suddenly by the ugly booger ever stayed the entire night.

In fact, no one ever spent a full night in the store. Oh, each person told his story, and everyone listened. People talked a lot about the ghost, about ways to outsmart it and about how surely the ultimate test of bravery would be to spend a full night with the Lineback ghost.

Some folks insisted on praying or singing religious songs or thinking only good thoughts when they had to walk past the store in the dark. Only a drunk dared to yell challenges at the ghost. No, this booger was real. Too many folks had seen and heard this one.

Philo Pritchard listened to all the talk. He never said much about the ghost, partly because Philo had a severe lisp and generally said as little as possible. But he thought about the haint every day.

After years of considering his level of bravery, Philo was at an age that he considered himself grown. And he had decided he was courageous enough to stay the whole night in the Lineback store. Why, he wasn't afraid of the devil himself. He would do it!

On the night of his test, Philo had been comfortably settled on the cot only a few minutes when the ghost appeared holding a small brass tallow lamp with a wick. Philo, wide-eyed and frozen by fear, watched and waited as the ghost slowly approached the cot. It was several minutes, an eternity for Philo, before the ghost spoke.

"I see there are two of us here tonight."

"Yeth, by God, and if you wait until I can get my panths on there will only be one of uth," said Philo who promptly pulled on his trousers and ran out of the store.

He kept running until he could no longer run. He stopped at a creek to get some water and restore his breath. As he was leaning over the creek he heard the ghost at his right shoulder.

"Well, we have had quite a race, haven't we?"

"Yeth, and if you wait until I get my thecond wind we will have another."

N.A.

THE CURSE ON DEAVER'S SPRINGS

About six miles west of Asheville, N. C. there is a sulphur spring which was known for many years as Deaver's Springs. Here, one of the most famous hotels in the South once provided recreation and recuperation for its guests. Following the Civil War, hundreds of wealthy Southerners came each summer to "take the waters." The scenery then, as now, was breathtaking, and within a decade, Deaver's Springs became noted for its mineral baths.

The famed springs were near the western bank of Caney Branch, a small stream that enters Hominy Creek, noted for its convoluted "double horseshoe" riverbed which abruptly curves north and east as it sweeps on towards the French Broad. This is the setting of one of the most peculiar legends in western North Carolina.

During the early part of this century, local residents of Deaver's Springs would point to an ancient white oak, calling it the "Township Tree." The consensus of local opinion was that the tree had stood there for more than two centuries. Children were told that the mound near the tree was the grave of a Cherokee warrior. According to local legend, the Cherokee's soul was still within the tree. When prompted by their elders, children would approach the tree quietly, knock on the great trunk and then whisper, "Cherokee warrior, what did you die for?"

Then, if the child placed his or her ear against the tree, the sad, plaintive answer would come: "Nothing at all."

Local residents have numerous stories about the consequences of this ritual. Disappointed children would tell their parents, "I did what you told me, and I heard nothing at all," to which the rejoinder was, "Didn't I tell you that you would hear the Indian say nothing at all?" There are variations, of course. Sometimes, older children would hide near the tree, and at the proper moment, they would give the harsh, whispered answer, "Noooothing, at all."

How did such a tradition originate?

Foster Sondley, author of the two-volume *History of Buncombe County*, remembers rapping on the Township Tree as a child. In later years, he talked to the oldest members of the community and learned an amazing story. The Indian buried by the Township Tree was allegedly part of a Cherokee war party. "When?" asked Sondley.

"Why, back when General Rutherford burned the Cherokee villages and destroyed their corn. Back in the seventeen-seventies."

Did he die in battle? asked Sondley.

"Oh, no! He was poisoned. That is why he put the curse on the spring!" Sondley's curiosity was piqued. He wanted to know more. It was many years before he knew it all, and in the end he found that the curse even affected him personally.

The Cherokee's name was Cheesquiah. He had come with two companions to the Hominy to spy on General Rutherford. He hoped to learn the size of the American's forces and the direction of their movement. Knowing this, Cheesquiah and his friend, Tahquittee, intended to relay their knowledge to a Cherokee war party. Cheesquiah had good cause to hate General Rutherford. The people of his village were dying of starvation. The young brave had seen the green corn trampled by the army's horses and cattle, and he had watched the soldiers torch the storage houses of winter provender. Like many other young braves, Cheesquiah burned with a need to strike a decisive blow against the white General.

The legend relates that Rutherford's forces had no idea that they were being observed, but the American did worry about the wolves. Packs followed in their wake, and at night the wolves attacked the cattle, Rutherford's primary food supply. When the soldiers poisoned the spring, it was in the hope that the wolves would come to drink. But the first to be poisoned was not a wolf. It was Cheesquiah. Unwittingly, he knelt and drank before returning to his two companions who crouched in the dark woods above him.

When Cheesquiah realized that the soldiers had poisoned the spring, his heart was filled with an indescribable rage. It was not his approaching death that angered him, but that he would die so ignobly. Poisoned! Not in the heat of battle, but helpless and convulsing. Cheesquiah managed to crawl to the thicket where his friends were concealed. There, he died, hidden in the undergrowth near the great white oak.

As his final agony seized him, Cheesquiah cursed the spring. "Nothing shall prosper here," he said. "From this day forth, the waters and the land of this place are cursed. He who lives here, let his heart be burdened. Distrust and envy seize him! Let prosperity elude him. May he live to curse his God and drink the bitter drink of despair!"

His friends buried him sitting up, facing the spring that had killed him. In later years, as they sat in the lodges of the Cherokees in Chota and Tenase, they told the story. Indeed, according to Sondley, an old Cherokee living in Graham County in 1881 repeated the tale to Sondley's grandfather, Robert Henry. (See "Iona's Son")

"How do you know this story is true?" said Henry.

"Because I was there," said the ancient Cherokee. "I am Tahquittee, kinsman of Yonagusta and friend to Cheesquiah." Then the old man smiled at Henry and said, "Cheesquiah's curse! Have you not reason to believe that it has been fulfilled?" Ruefully, Henry, who had once invested in Deaver's Springs, acknowledged that he did.

In the latter part of his life, Foster Sondley published an undated, sixteen-page monograph called *The Indian's Curse*. The following quote is especially noteworthy. Speaking of himself in the third person, Sondley says:

The gentleman who has preserved this tradition is himself a member of the family that owned the place longer than any other and suffered most of them all. ... All of this preceded many of the grave and singular sufferings which have come to those who owned or controlled the site. The peculiar afflictions of such persons have long been observed and are a frequent subject of comment in the vicinity as an unparalleled verification of a remarkable malediction.

Elsewhere, Sondley is more specific.

The curse seems to have been in great measure realized.

For about half of the time which has elapsed since its occupation by whites began, the property so cursed has been in litigation Some of the suits have been between members of the same family, and many of them protracted, expensive and bitter. Those who have claimed the spring...have been subject to serious misfortunes. Financial ruin, law suits, domestic infelicities, separations, divorces, brawls, violent deaths, fires, insanities, suicides, shipwrecks, family quarrels and other distresing [sic] afflictions have been so frequent occurence among them that almost no one has escaped the vengeance which apparently impended over all concerned in the location. One owner alone, in addition to numerous other dire calamities, had eighteen houses burned on it while it belonged to him.

Sondley goes on to say that of all the curses he has encountered in literature and history, this one surpasses all others in both "malignity of its imprecation and the magnitude of its fulfillment." It is possible that no other spot on the American continent has such a record of disaster.

The spring still exists, and although the name has been changed many times, tragedy and misfortune have continued. The number of hotels which have burned is especially alarming. As Sondley concludes, "To the superstitious it exceeds mere coincidence and becomes a case of fearful retributions."

G.C./N.A.

THE GRINDER

In the early part of the 19th century, a writer named Charles Lanman traveled deep into the Southern Highlands searching for stories that would capture the imagination of his readers. Lanman had a particular penchant for what he called "the unusual" — something that suggested the dark and savage history of the region. He would often ask where the oldest resident lived, for these were the people who remembered "the old time."

One wintry evening near Toccoa, Georgia, Lanman heard of an Indian rumored to be more than one-hundred years old. "He remembers a world before white people," said the informant who led the writer to a strange, mound-like shelter. The entry was so small that Lanman found it necessary to get down on his hands and knees to crawl inside. The old Indian's eyes glinted in the firelight, and as Lanman's companion acted as interpreter, the writer asked the old Cherokee to tell him something of the time before the white man came.

The old man spoke with a measured cadence, pausing to let the interpreter translate. Lanman wrote. He wrote all night, recording the old man's memories of teeming wildlife, voices that spoke to his people in the wind, and of heroic deeds long forgotten. Among the tales that Lanman recorded is the story of the place beneath a great waterfall the Cherokees called "the cauldron."

In the ancient past, the Cherokees had once lived to the north in a place near a great river that flowed into the sea. But there had been a war with the

Delawares, and after more than a decade of fighting, the Cherokees retreated south. Crossing the blue mountains, they finally stopped, settling in the deep coves and valleys of the mountains called the Unakas. But the Delawares were relentless. In a bitterness born out of years of fighting, they pursued their enemy, "the Tsalaghis," determined to not merely defeat them but to annihilate them. In time, the tide turned, and the Cherokees established a boundary. "Do not come beyond the blue mountains," they told the "Anakwanki," the Delawares. "This is our home now."

Warfare became sporadic, but the enmity between the two tribes did not lessen. Too many fathers, brothers and sons had died on both sides. The blood oath of retribution flourished. So, there came an evening when a Cherokee war party returned to the Toccoa townhouse with a dozen prisoners. Moving through the village, the Cherokee war party taunted their prisoners.

"Look about you, Delawares," said the warriors. "See the faces. Widows, mothers, sons and daughters of those you have killed. They will make you dance and beg tonight!" they said laughing.

The young Delawares, tied with leather thongs, attempted a show of bravado, staring coolly at the angry faces about them. At the townhouse, they were pushed inside where the Cherokee elders sat. Although they understood little of what was said, the Delawares knew that these old men were debating their fate. The talk was long and heated, but finally one who spoke their language told them, "We may not kill you, Delaware. Perhaps we will exchange you for our friends who were taken prisoner by you."

The Delawares were silent. Did the Cherokees not know that all prisoners taken by the Delaware were burned at the stake? Thus had been the fate of the Cherokees taken prisoner only days before.

Finally, one with a sly face and a twisted mouth said, "How will you tell our war-chief of this?"

"We will release one of you to carry the message," said the elder. And so it was. The thongs were cut, and as he was led from the townhouse, the prisoner with the sly face called out, "Go quickly, brother — and return quickly as well!"

30

The elders called an old woman named Walini and told her that the care of the Delawares was entrusted to her. "You have lost a husband to the Delaware," they said, "but perhaps your son who we believe is a Delaware prisoner will be returned to you." Walini nodded.

The prisoners were kept within a lodge near the townhouse. The old woman fed the men a meager diet of bread and water. Each day she checked their bonds, loosening those that inhibited circulation and tightening those that appeared too loose. The man with the sly face spoke to her softly, requesting more food or the removal of the leather thongs. Walini did not answer. When she was gone, he would tell the others, "Our brothers will come in the night to free us before the moon is full. We must be ready. Let us try to convince the old woman to untie us, for we must be able to move quickly when the time comes."

And so, each day they appealed to Walini, conveying with gestures and facial expressions what they could not say in Cherokee. "You remind me of my own mother," said the sly one. "Will I see her again?" The others pretended pain and discomfort, pointing to their hands and feet, begging her for help. Walini said nothing, moving among them with corn mush and water, testing the bonds.

One evening when she arrived at the prisoners' lodge, Walini saw a young Cherokee boy waiting for her. "The enemy is in the next valley," he said. "I fear that there are no prisoners to exchange, and they have come to rescue their friends." The boy gestured towards the hillside nearby saying, "We are ready for them. I have come to help you move the prisoners."

Walini stood for a moment considering what the boy had told her. "Go," she said. "I need no help."

Entering the lodge, she was immediately surrounded by pleas and hypocritical smiles. The prisoners sensed something was happening — perhaps their rescue was imminent. A chorus of supplication rose, and then fell into silence when she raised her hand.

Her face spoke for her. "Yes," it said, "I will release you." Then with gestures she indicated that they must do as she said. With a stick in the dirt,

31

she drew a trail that led to the north. She mimicked silence and stealth, showing them how they must move. Then she told them to strip, indicating that the Cherokees must find no trace of them. Using torn strips of their clothing, she bound the prisoners together.

"We are going through the dark now ... down this darkened trail. This is so none of you will become lost." Then she tore more strips, indicating that they must be blindfolded. "We don't want you returning with a great war party to kill us all in our sleep," she mimed. They smiled and nodded, looking furtively at each other as she bound their eyes.

When Walini led the Delawares from the lodge, the moon was hidden in a cloud bank. Thunder muttered and drops of cold rain began to fall. Walini goaded the first man into a trot and the entire line followed, bound to one another. They went through the chilling rain, trotting down the narrow trail. They were trembling now, but it would have been difficult to tell if they were reacting to the bitter rain or the anticipation of freedom. The sly-faced one smiled crookedly as he sensed a change in their surroundings. Tree limbs no longer raked across his naked flesh and a current of air washed across him. The trail no longer led upwards.

Walini halted the procession. Turning, she looked at the smiling, expectant face of the sly one, he who had struggled the hardest to deceive her. Then she tore away the blindfold, dropping it to waft downwards into the boiling waters of a mountain gorge. While his eyes struggled to comprehend, she sent him over the edge. And so they fell, each dragging his companion after him, falling through the torrent of a great waterfall into a jagged bowl of rock. The Cherokee called it "the cauldron" or "the grinder," for it was much like the churning action of the device they used to grind corn. Relentlessly, the waters pounded down. Nothing could withstand the endless action, neither wood, stone, flesh nor bone.

The screams of the Delawares were lost in the thunderous roar of water. "They have their freedom at last," Walini told herself. "Perhaps in time many of their brothers will join them."

...In the fading light Charles Lanman looked at the face of the old Cherokee as he leaned forward and spoke in a harsh whisper. Lanman waited for the translation.

"Sometimes, you white men argue about the white mineral that coats the great rocks around 'the cauldron.' 'It could be soapstone,' you say, or some kind of chalk." The old man grinned, revealing toothless gums.

N.A./G.C.

THE WAYWARD GATE

*A word of caution, traveler. In the
land beyond the Wayward Gate, Reason
sleeps while Dreams move and speak.*
— The Wayward Gate

When the first settlers on our eastern seaboard heard rumors about the rich spoils to the west, they began to search for an easy passage. There were countless stories of frustration and hardship. Impatient farmers from Virginia and the coasts of the Carolinas and Georgia found themselves lost in laurel hells and cul de sacs. Forced to retrace their steps down rugged mountainsides, they warned the newcomers. "Turn back. That way lies Hell for Certain, Misery Knob and Bitter Acres." There had to be an easier route. There was.

Finally, the word spread: "Follow the rivers." Settlers en route to Tennessee and Kentucky learned that five of the rivers in the Carolinas meandered southeast. All penetrated the Blue Ridge and gave easy access to the rich river valleys beyond. One however was especially appealing: Chimney Rock Pass. Through it ran an ancient Indian trail used by the Cherokees and the Catawbas, and the first settlers that ventured through this six-mile gateway found it to be an enchanted country. The river was a continuous cascade filled with deep pools and great stone cliffs on either side of the gorge ranged from two-hundred feet to half a mile wide. Everywhere there were strange rock formations carved by wind, water and ancient glaciers. The great stone column which quickly acquired the name of Chimney Rock stood like a sentinel above the gorge; caves abounded, as did breathtaking views. It was as though all that the mountains had to offer in terms of grandeur and spectacle had been concentrated in the few square miles of this mountain pass. There was something otherworldly about it.

Perhaps too much so. The first settlers who moved up Broad River through Chimney Rock Pass and on into Swannanoa became uneasy in the gorge. The light seemed unusual, especially at twilight. Distance between objects became uncertain and the air seemed to shimmer. Those pools were beautiful, but weights lowered into them, hammers and axes on long lengths of rope, never touched bottom. And the wind. Well, it was gentle and cooling, but the sound was unusual. Visitors characterized it as musical and concluded that it had something to do with the stone formations. The wind seemed to move through them like an Aeolian harp, producing strange thrumming melodies.

Often there was another, less musical sound, like distant thunder, which seemed to emanate from a nearby bald. Occasionally, great boulders would come thundering down the mountainside and crash into the river where thousands of others lay. Clouds of smoke or dust floated above the peak that the settlers eventually named Rumbling Bald. An early scientist who passed through Chimney Rock Pass characterized the region as restless, explaining that some of the oldest geological formations in the world are here. There are areas of significant instability, he said, adding that perhaps Rumbling Bald marks the site of an ancient volcano. Other scientists have made similar observations, noting that there is a perfectly logical explanation for falling rocks, internal thunder and "singing stones." Local residents were chided for calling the pools "bottomless." Their depth can be measured scientifically, they were told. Apparently, one of the pools is more than one-hundred feet deep.

But there are other mysteries.

Early settlers living in the area of Chimney Rock Pass, now Hickory Nut Gap, have seen a variety of strange apparitions. Take Patsy Reaves, for example:

...a widow woman, who lives near the Appalachian Mountain declared that on the 31st day of July last (1806) about six o'clock p.m., her daughter, Elizabeth, about eight years old, was in the cotton field, about ten poles from the dwelling house, which stands by computation, six furloughs from Chimney Mountain, and that Elizabeth told her brother, Morgan, aged 11 years, that there was a man on the mountain. Morgan was incredulous at first; but the little girl affirmed it and said she saw him rolling rocks and picking up sticks, adding that she saw a heap of people. Morgan then went to the place she was and called out, said that he saw a thousand things flying in the air. On which, Polly, daughter of Mrs. Reaves, aged 14 years, and a Negro woman, ran to the children and called to Mrs. Reaves to come and see what a sight yonder was. Mrs. Reaves says she went about 8 poles toward them, and without any sensible alarm or fright, she turned toward the Chimney Mountains and discovered a very numerous croud (sic) of beings resembling the human species; but could not discern any particular members of the human body, nor distinction of sexes; that they were of every size, from the tallest man down to the least infant; that there were more of the small than of the full grown; that they appeared to rise off the side of the mountain south of said rock and about as high; that a considerable part of the mountain's top was visible above their shining host; that they moved in a northern direction and collected about the top of the Chimney rock. When all but a few had reached said rock, two seemed to rise together, and behind them about two feet, a third rose. These three rose with great agility toward the croud and had the nearest resemblance to men of any before seen. While beholding these three, her eyes were attracted by three more rising nearly from the same place, and moving swiftly in the same order and direction. After these, several others rose and went toward the rock.

During this view, which all the spectators tho't lasted upwards of an hour, she sent for Mr. Robert Siercy, who did not come at first; on a second message sent about fifteen minutes after the first Mr. Siercy came; and being now before us, he gave the following relation, to the substance of which Mrs. Reaves agrees:

Mr. Siercy says that when he was coming he expected to see nothing extraordinary, and when he come, being asked if he saw those people on the mountain, he said "no", but on looking a second time he saw more glittering white appearance of human kind than ever he had seen of men at any general review; that they were of all sizes, from that of men to infants; that they moved in throngs about a large rock, not far from the Chimney rock; that they were about the height of the Chimney rock and moved in a semi-circular course between him and the mountain to the place where Mrs. Reaves said they rose; and that two of a full size went before the general croud about the space of twenty yards; and as they respectively came to this place, they vanished out of sight, leaving a solemn and pleasing impression on the mind, accompanied with diminution of bodily strength.

The preceding account was written by George Newton, a Presbyterian minister who noted that possibly this event was a prelude to "the descent of the Holy City." In a post script, he added that on the same day another resident living several miles away observed a rainbow in the vicinity of the Chimney despite the fact that there was no indication of clouds or rain. The resident speculated about the possibility that some form of moisture emanated from the mountain, thus producing a rainbow.

Several years later, an elderly couple living in the gap of what is called Chimney Rock Falls witnessed another apparition, this time a ghostly battle. On a succession of evenings as the old couple watched the sunlight fade on the mountain summits, they had seen two armies approach each other across the sky. The witnesses also heard the command to attack and watched a phantom cavalry charge. The heavens reverberated with hoofbeats, cries of pain and the clash of swords. Then, darkness eclipsed the scene.

Prompted by the credibility of the witnesses, the town of Rutherfordton called a public meeting. They decided to ask the old couple to repeat their experience for an official delegation consisting of two generals, a magistrate and a clerk. The witnesses complied and dutifully signed affidavits. The story of the spectral battle was widely published in regional newspapers (1811). The story was still popular in the 1880's when Wilber Zeigler and Ben Grosscup passed through the region and recorded it for their travel book, *Heart of the Alleghanies.*

So, what are we to make of all this? Are there "more things in heaven and earth than are dreamt of" in our experience? Consider this story from ancient Cherokee tradition.

The Cherokees believed the strange land beyond the rock pillar to be associated with magic. Called "Suwali-nuna" or the Suwali Trail, it was a portion of a trading path that ran along the Swannanoa River and then passed through the Gorge. The Cherokees used it when they traded with eastern tribes such as the Catawba and Sara. It was the path they took to seek "tsa-lu," the sacred tobacco plant.

In Cherokee mythology, the Gorge that ran below the rock pillar was inhabited by magical beings. Here were water spirits and giant hawks, serpents and invisible spirits; but most significantly, here in this wind-washed gorge lived the "Yunwi Tsundsdi," the "little people."

There are hundreds of myths about the Cherokee "wee folk," and in the majority of instances they are depicted as benevolent but mischievous beings. However, such is not the case with those living in the gorge beyond the stone pillar. Perceiving themselves as the guardians of the sacred tobacco plant, they warned the Cherokees that they would kill anyone who passed through their land in search of tsa-lu. And so it was. The Cherokees sent their swiftest warriors and their most powerful medicine men. If they were not destroyed by the crashing boulders that the little people rolled from the mountaintops, they died when raging winds cast them into deep waters. Since the Yundi Tsundsdi had magical powers, they could transform themselves into other forms: eagles, whirlwinds and giant fish. But finally, a Cherokee shaman transformed himself into a humming bird which flew unobserved through the land of the Yundi Tsundsdi and stole the sacred tobacco. Returning through the gorge, he became a mighty wind and destroyed the little people and their homes. When he was back in the village of the Cherokee, the people greeted him as their savior. He gave them tsa-lu, the magic plant that cured their illness, protected them from evil and enabled them to foretell the future.

In later years, when the Cherokee traveled the Suwali trail, they were unchallenged. But the Yundi Tsundsdi were still there. Sometimes, in the spring or summer, Cherokee hunters told of seeing them dressed in their white ceremonial clothes that they only wore on special occasions. According to one legend, so many of them traveled to the top of the great stone pillar, it appeared that its crest was covered with snow. One wonders if they flew to the summit as the shimmering beings did on that summer day in 1806 when Polly Reaves called her mother to see "what a sight yonder was."

In 1874 Old Rumbling Bald became Quaking Bald. For six months the eastern end of the mountain shook. Plates rattled in their shelves all over the valley; window frames shook themselves to pieces. The citizenry of Rutherfordton seventeen miles away listened anxiously to the subterranean quakes and watched their dishes dance on the table. Cascades of rubble and boulders crashed down the mountain. Some local residents went on lengthy visits to relatives in Asheville, and an itinerant preacher held a revival in the Gorge that netted twenty-five converts. Rumors spread about an awakening volcano and impending eruptions. Local folks speculated about the direction of the lava flow.

Again, the scientists arrived, smiled tolerantly and assured everyone that lava was not forthcoming. "You are witnessing a change in the mountain's topography," they said. "Great masses of rock are shifting; the elasticity of ledges is stressed. When they shatter, boulders shift and fall within the mountain."

To prove their point, the scientists clammered up the one-thousand foot face of the mountain and crawled through fissures. "Just as we thought," they said as they emerged, brushing the dirt from their clothes. "There are great hollow caves in there that act as sounding boards which magnify sound like an echo chamber. Nothing to worry about."

"What about the smoke?"

"That isn't smoke. That is dust." Chastened, the local residents returned home. Before the quakes abated, one-hundred separate shocks were recorded.

Nature's antics in Hickory Nut Gorge are sporadic, but always, as though reasserting its mysterious nature, something will eventually happen. In the 1930's the "singing stones" returned. However, there was a difference.

"I don't think it is the wind," said one witness. "I have heard the music several times, now, and I believe it is coming from within the mountain." This was not a singular testimony. Numerous people heard the sound ... far too many to dismiss. Curious journalists arrived.

"What does it sound like?" The answers varied. "Soft and quavering" or "beautiful" but always "weird." There are intervals of silence between the "songs."

"Are there voices singing?"

"No. At least not human voices."

Eventually they stopped.

Hickory Nut Gorge has been silent for a long time. Scientists came and again measured the bottomless pools. The unusual depth had been produced by the scouring action of pebbles that had gradually worn away the stone. They advanced theories about "mirage" conditions that would explain the ghostly battle and the people who appeared to fly to the top of Chimney Rock. Similar apparitions had been seen in Wales and Switzerland, they said, droning on about "refraction" and "cold air mass."

Life has become somewhat prosaic along the Suwali Trail. People no longer sit in hushed groups around the base of Chimney Rock waiting for "the sound of music." Even Zeigler and Grossup said that Bat Cave was a disappointment. Enjoy the beauty and tranquility of the Gorge, they said. Don't make the difficult climb to Bat Cave. It is just a gloomy and unremarkable cavern. (Some local historians have indicated that visitors to the cave often mistake the antechamber for the actual Bat Cave, not realizing that one of the majestic caves of the Southeast lies just beyond the back wall.) The locals no longer recommend it. "Snakes," they say. "Not many bats in there now. Why don't you take a dip in the bottomless pools." And lots of people do, bobbing and laughing in the waters that had once inspired awe and reflection in early settlers. The Gorge is still beautiful, of course. There is Lake Lure, the grandeur of mountain scenery, the azure sky. Hikers, fishermen and honeymooners crowd the banks of Rocky Broad, staring at the great boulders. Bird song, soft breezes and spectacular sunsets.

Has it been tamed? Is the wildness and magic gone, or is Hickory Nut Gorge just waiting for us to become inattentive, to doze off in the sun?

G.C.

New Hanover County Public Library
Main Library
7/12/2014

Thank you for using self check-out

Total... 6642

34200002224934
Get... (BC) Hoaxes and hustlers /
Date Due: 07/23/2014 11:58:00 PM

34200002099490
See... (BC) ... on roman...
Date Due: 07/22/2014 11:59:00 PM

34200002197382
... (BC) How to handle...
Date Due: 07/23/2014 11:59:00 PM

34200002199234
See... (BC) ...
Date Due: 07/23/2014 11:59:00 PM

34200002369274
See... (BC) The vanishing hitchhiker...
Date Due: 07/23/2014 11:59:00 PM

34200002131240
See... (BC) The day you...
??? until Saturday?
Date Due: 7/23/2014 11:59:00 PM

34200002268272
See... (BC) The truth never stands in the
way of a good story /
Date Due: 07/23/2014 11:59:00 PM

34200002092732
See... (BC) Bald buzzards, bushbabies and
growing anaconda...
Date Due: 07/23/2014 11:59:00 PM

Monday and Tuesday 9 A.M. to 8 P.M.
Wednesday and Thursday 9 A.M. to 6 P.M.
Friday and Saturday 9 A.M. to 5 P.M.
Telephone Renewals: 910-798-6320
Website: www.nhclibrary.org
Checked Out / # Not Checked Out
8/0

New Hanover County Public Library
Main Library
7/2/2014

Thank you for using self-checkout!

**********5862

34200003254949
Sec- (BC): Hoaxers and hustlers /
Date Due: 07/23/2014 11:59:00 PM

34200005966680
Sec- (BC): You can't cheat an honest man :
Date Due: 07/23/2014 11:59:00 PM

34200005183443
Sec- (BC): Holy homicide :
Date Due: 07/23/2014 11:59:00 PM

34200002139034
Sec- (BC): Curses, broiled again! :
Date Due: 07/23/2014 11:59:00 PM

34200000369278
Sec- (BC): The vanishing hitchhiker :
Date Due: 07/23/2014 11:59:00 PM

34200007651280
Sec- (BC): The baby on the car roof and
222 more urban legends /
Date Due: 07/23/2014 11:59:00 PM

34200006166272
Sec- (BC): The truth never stands in the
way of a good story /
Date Due: 07/23/2014 11:59:00 PM

34200005025792
Sec- (BC): Belled buzzards, hucksters and
grieving specters :
Date Due: 07/23/2014 11:59:00 PM

Monday and Tuesday 9 A.M to 8 P.M.
Wednesday and Thursday 9 A.M. to 6 P.M.
Friday and Saturday 9 A.M. to 5 P.M.
Telephone Renewals: 910-798-6320
Website: www.nhclibrary.org
Checked Out / # Not Checked Out
8 / 0

PART II

MURDER, MAYHEM AND GALLOWS DRAMA

INTRODUCTION

My race is run
Beneath the sun,
The gallows waits for me.
—— traditional refrain in numerous folk ballads

In the last quarter of the 19th century, a unique form of journalism developed in the Southern Highlands. The majority of regional news was reported on the "Editorial Page" via letters. Prior to the advent of correspondents and regional reporters, editors customarily published letters from ministers, teachers and other highly literate professionals who gave eyewitness accounts of local events. Frequently such letters were unabashedly self-serving. Politicians lauded the "salubrious beauties," a favorite phrase, of their region, stressing the healthy environs, mineral deposits and economic potential; retired teachers waxed nostalgic about one-room schools, and friends of recently deceased notables gave glowing accounts, replete with verse eulogies of the life and final hours of the dearly departed.

Perhaps the most lengthy narratives were devoted to first-hand accounts of executions. These events were usually publicized months in advance, and were frequently attended by thousands of people. Although judged macabre by modern standards, executions quickly evolved into social occasions, complete with picnic lunches, ministers who spoke from the scaffold, and large numbers of young "sparking couples." Such a colorful gathering was certainly a challenge to a writer's skill; however, capable reporters seemed to be plentiful. No doubt, the varied details of scores of execution day events passed into oblivion for want of a Boswell. However, in many instances, newspapers continued to carry letters from the witnesses to grim justice for months after the event.

Most of these reports follow a curious format. The writer begins by assuring his readers that he was not a willful spectator at this distasteful affair, but had stumbled on it while on his way to a nature outing or a cultural presentation. On learning he had come upon an execution, he invariably announces his intention of leaving, but his less sensitive friends and companions insist on staying. Consequently, he decides to make the best of the occasion by recording a detailed account. He finds the behavior of the crowd insensitive and morbid, but frequently manages to interview both the condemned and the attending law officials.

Based on numerous accounts of executions in small mountain communities, there is substantial evidence that the majority of witnesses at executions did not deserve to be characterized as morbid and insensitive. Curious and perceiving the event as an adventure, they traveled to the gallows site in much the same manner as they would have gone to a county fair. This conclusion seems to be borne out by their behavior before and after the execution.

In a letter describing the execution of Dave Mason of Haywood County, N.C., who was hanged in Asheville in 1852, the writer mentions the behavior of the spectators. From a festive atmosphere filled with laughter and shouts, the crowd was suddenly transformed to a panic-stricken mob. As frequently happened, Mason's drop through the trap-door did not kill him. As his death throes continued, women began to weep and the sound of moaning filled the air. According to Clark Medford, a Haywood County historian, it was a cold, windy day in October and the moaning of the wind mingled with the sighs and weeping of the distraught audience. The people dispersed quickly, within minutes; nothing remained except the executioner and the corpse. "Ohhhhhhh," said the wind that swayed the corpse; "Ohhhhhhh" wailed the retreating crowd. Peter Mason, the dead man's father, placed his son in a wagon and drove forty miles to Crabtree Community in Haywood County. It was dark when he got his son home.

In many accounts of the final moments of the condemned, the writer notes the confusion and shock of the spectators when they are confronted by an ugly reality--a dying man twisting in the air. It is as though nothing had prepared the audience for the brutal horror of the actual event. There were exceptions, of course; hardened farmers who yelled humorous quips, women who raptly watched the event with something akin to hunger, undisciplined children who clamored up the gallows steps. But the majority seemed to suffer the same rude awakening when the body dropped through the trapdoor. One wonders, what did they expect?

G.C.

THE HANGING OF
BAYLESS HENDERSON

During the summer of 1873, a small band of teachers and ministers set out to visit a number of educational institutions in western North Carolina. The group's purpose was to ascertain the quality of education available in the "seminaries and Sabbath schools" of the region. Traditionally, the group arrived for commencement programs and attended classes in which students underwent oral examinations.

On the morning of June 6, 1873, the group departed from Hicksville, "pleased and edified" by the "victory over ignorance" that the schools were waging in that community. Passing through Macon County, they traveled on towards Jackson's county seat, the little village of Webster. Approaching the court house, the travelers were surprised to see Webster's streets and houses crowded with people of "almost every sex, age and color." Inquiring as to the reason for this massive gathering, they were told that the murderer, Bayless Henderson, was to be hanged in the village square. Indeed, preparations had been underway since daybreak.

The travelers seemed to take the grim proceedings in stride. Several set about recording the event for the *Carolina Citizen* in Asheville since eyewitness accounts of historic events were sought by most newspapers at the time. All records of the day's events estimate the number of witnesses as "in excess of 3,000." Further, the travelers learned that the majority of the people were from Jackson, Macon, Swain and Haywood counties. The large attendance was attributed to the prominence of Captain Nimrod S. Jarrett, the wealthy Macon County landowner who had been murdered by Henderson.

The atmosphere around the scaffold was frankly festive. The place of execution was immediately in front of the jail door and in full view of almost every resident of the village. Picnic baskets abounded and groups of young people strolled about the village streets. Many of the girls wore brightly colored summer dresses and their demeanor was at variance to the somber occasion. At 1 p.m., almost two hours before the scheduled execution, Henderson was conducted by Sheriff Bumgarner and Deputy Sheriff Allman to the scaffold where he took his seat before a vast crowd of spectators. Several ministers were also in attendance and took the opportunity to sing hymns and pray for the condemned man.

According to eyewitnesses, Henderson appeared to enjoy the proceedings. At one point, he rose and gave the audience a vivid account of his sinful past. Then, in what appeared to be a truly repentant manner, he cautioned all of the young men in the crowd to look at his condition and strive to avoid his fate. He urged them to shun evil ways and avoid dissipation. He confessed his guilt and acknowledged the justice of his sentence, adding that he had no fears concerning his immortal soul since he had "embraced religion some days past."

In endeavoring to accurately record facts regarding Henderson, one gentleman sought out and questioned friends or acquaintances of the condemned man. Most of them were skeptical about Henderson's new-found religion, adding that practically every statement Bayless had made to his captors concerning his origins and life prior to his arrival in North Carolina had proved to be false. Drawing near the scaffold, the recorder studied the condemned man's face. "He was a large young man," he wrote, "professing to be twenty-two years of age." The witness found this latter fact unlikely and stated that he would estimate his age as close to thirty. "He had lost an eye and claimed that it happened while he was in the army." This fact also appeared to be false since Henderson claimed to have served for ten years, yet he had been unable to produce any supportive evidence.

"Bayless Henderson was not only illiterate, he was ignorant," said his chronicler, almost destitute of intelligence and moral training, and his associations in life must have been of the lowest grade." All attempts to identify or contact relatives had failed. His own lawyer had been unable to learn anything about his client's origin other than he said he was from Tennessee — a detail which, according to one of his captors, accounted for Bayless's lack of moral or ethical principles. "It's like this," said one of Bayless's acquaintances, "Henderson will climb a tree to tell a lie when he could stand on the ground and tell the truth."

Many of the spectators later expressed amazement at the condemned man's behavior on the scaffold. He laughed frequently, nodded to friends and seemed to be particularly friendly to Sheriff Bumgarner, who was to be his executioner. In effect, he seemed eager to die. His good humor prompted several witnesses to express their doubts that Henderson fully understood the gravity of his situation.

How did this luckless man come to stand on a rough-hewn scaffold surrounded by a milling crowd, laughter and music? Is there anything in the accounts of his crime that give any insight into the man?

Nine months prior to his execution, Bayless Henderson had appeared in Macon County. He professed to be looking for work, but several local farmers observed that he didn't seem to be looking very hard. He was later described by witnesses as "a tramp." Some found his behavior furtive and felt he was probably a fugitive from justice — a desperado. He became a familiar figure as he trudged the roads between Franklin, Aquone and Nantahala. Occasionally, he could be seen lounging on the porch of a general store where he listened attentively to the local gossip. Doubtless, this is where he heard the name of Captain Nimrod S. Jarrett and learned that he lived nearby.

Rumored to be one of the wealthiest men in western North Carolina, Jarrett was a successful farmer, miner and road builder who owned extensive tracts of land in three counties. Now, at the age of seventy-two, he lived with his wife in Nantahala Valley and continued to oversee the operation of several businesses.

It is not surprising that Captain Jarrett was an object of both speculation and envy to some of his neighbors. As he rode to and from his holdings in Nantahala and Aquone (a portion of which he bought with William Holland Thomas, the white chief of the Cherokees), his passage was noted by his neighbors. Was he off to visit his orchards or his mining operation? Is it true that he owns stock in the "ginseng plant" in Haywood County? How much money do you suppose he carries in his saddle bags? Bayless Henderson listened attentively. Then, on the morning of September 15, 1872, he stationed himself several miles below the Jarrett home and waited. In his pocket was a single-barreled firearm that the court would later describe as a "two-dollar pistol."

Jarrett's wife had intended to accompany her husband as far as their daughter's home in Aquone while Jarrett continued on to Franklin. Becoming impatient with his wife's slowness, Jarrett finally announced that he would ride on, and his wife could catch up with him before he reached Aquone. So it was that Captain Jarrett saddled his horse and rode away from the home he named Apple Tree Farm. Riding by the Nantahala River, he approached a young man standing on the roadside. Jarrett greeted him, and as the stranger turned his face up, smiling, the Captain probably noted that he was blind in one eye. Allegedly, Henderson asked if he might ride behind the Captain to Aquone, and Jarrett complied.

Within moments of her husband's departure, Mrs. Jarrett was riding briskly toward Aquone. She found her husband face down on the road, and seeing the fatal wound in the back of his head, she resisted the urge to dismount and immediately rode for help. Returning with a group of neighbors, Mrs. Jarrett searched the woods for her husband's horse. One of Jarrett's neighbors called attention to a number of footprints around the body. Due to the softness of the earth, the prints were detailed and distinctive.

"It would be easy to match a print like that!" said a neighbor.

At this point, a stranger joined the group. Standing outside the circle, he craned his neck, attempting to see the footprints. Several men turned their attention to the new arrival, noting his trousers were wet to the knees.

"I was on the other side of the river, and I waded over to see what had happened," explained the stranger.

"You wouldn't mind showing us your shoes, would you?"

"My shoes didn't make them prints, if that's what you mean. Why, my shoes don't even have heels!" At this point, the stranger showed his shoe soles. The heels were missing from both shoes and appeared to have been recently pried off. After a whispered consultation, the neighbors encircled the bedraggled man and seized him. A quick search produced a cheap pistol which showed evidence of having been fired recently.

"Who are you?" asked one of the neighbors.

"I'm Bayless Henderson," he said. Then, as an afterthought, he added, "I'm from Tennessee."

At this point, all the evidence against Bayless Henderson was circumstantial; however, it was compelling. The shoes, despite the removal of the heels, matched the prints around Jarrett's body. Ironically, the most damning fact was the missing heels. To Jarrett's neighbors, their removal was a blatant and simple-minded attempt to obscure guilt. Bayless was taken to Franklin and imprisoned. The following day, he was indicted for murder in the first degree and his trial was set for the December term of court. Bayless' court-appointed attorneys immediately asked for a change of venue on the grounds that an impartial jury could not be found in Macon County. The request was granted and the trial was set for Webster, the county seat of Jackson County, on December 18. The trial lasted a single day.

At the conclusion of the trial, Bayless' attorney, William L. Norwood, made a feeble attempt to have the verdict set aside on the grounds that his client was accused of killing "one N.S. Jarrett" whereas the deceased was named "Nimrod S. Jarrett." The presiding judge, James Henry, son of Robert Henry (see "Iona's Son"), promptly overruled Norwoods' motion.

Despite Judge Henry's ruling, Henderson seized on the variations in Jarrett's name as his only defense. Dismissing his attorneys, he informed the court that he felt his defense had been poorly handled. Moreover, new evidence had come to his attention. Judge Henry denied Henderson's plea and pronounced the sentence of death by hanging. From his cell in Webster, Bayless wrote a personal appeal to the State Supreme Court. His appeal was granted.

Henderson's personal appeal remains the single most mystifying aspect of this story. The letter was not written by an illiterate and ignorant man. Indeed, it seems fair to indicate that if the appeal was written by Henderson, it reveals him to be a man of education and intelligence. Why would he conceal such a fact? Yet, in the final consideration, Bayless had no new evidence. Once more, he recounted the differences between Jarrett's names. With admirable patience, Judge Thomas Settle upheld Judge Henry's verdict, explaining in a lengthy and somewhat pedantic statement that people were often known by their initials, and that "Nimrod S. Jarrett" and N.S. Jarrett were undoubtedly the same person.

Upon learning that his appeal had failed, Bayless planned and executed an escape from the Webster jail. Remembering that the condemned man claimed to be a native of Tennessee, Sheriff Bumgarner concentrated his search to the west of Webster and captured Henderson within hours of his escape. The posse found him hiding beneath a brush pile.

Shortly after his return to the Webster jail, Bayless confessed, providing details of the murder that had not been resolved. Jarrett's gold watch was retrieved from a tree stump where Bayless had hidden it. The robbery had been unsuccessful because Jarrett's money was in his saddlebags and the horse had run away. Henderson had been forced to flee the scene when he heard the sound of Mrs. Jarrett's horse approaching. There was nothing left to tell.

And so, we return to the scaffold in Webster. "Whatever may have been his moral state or spiritual consolations, one thing is certain," wrote one of the chroniclers. "He met his fate with all its dreadful surroundings with as much composure and submission as I have ever witnessed in any person." Henderson's final act before the rope was placed around his neck was to thank all those who had been kind to him. He was especially enthusiastic in his appreciation of the kindness of Sheriff Bumgarner and his deputy. This opinion was shared by one of the spectators who wrote the *Carolina Citizen* the following week. "Bumgarner's arrangements to preserve order and solemnity in such a large and promiscuous assembly certainly entitle him to the approbation of all concerned."

Henderson's face was covered and his arms bound at his sides. A strong, small rope was placed around his neck and tied to a beam that was twelve feet above the ground. When he fell, he was suspended half-way between the beam and the earth. An attending physician noted that the plunge did not break Henderson's neck, but that "the rope was so deeply embedded in his flesh that respiration, circulation and sensation were cut off as with a lightning stroke." The body did not contort or struggle. "A trembling as from a slight chill passed over him about two minutes after he dropped." Some curious spectators made their way to the rude scaffold and stared at the corpse, but the majority silently turned and made their way home like some vast congregation that had witnessed an event that gave them much to ponder. Indeed, Henderson's departure from this world may have been the sole moment in his reckless and thoughtless existence when he managed to provoke introspection in others. For a brief moment, others had looked to him for guidance.

G.C.

Note: As a child, Gary Carden listened raptly to All Hallow's Eve tales — stories about headless farmers who wandered the moon-lit Balsam mountains, drowned babes loudly protesting their murder by cruel, immoral girls. One tale dealt with Bayless. It seems that prior to the 20th century physicians had little or no recourse to cadavers. Given the laws and strictures of the time, the only opportunity for the acquisition of such a resource was the death of those "unknelled and unknown." The newspapers of this period frequently carried stories of grave-robbing, and occasionally, an embarrassed physician was caught in the act. Public reaction to such pilfering was tempered by the fact that the victim rarely had friends or relatives in the community. Physicians wisely selected the graves of unidentified tramps or persons whose passing went unnoticed. Such was Bayless Henderson. The Halloween story has it that the luckless Tennessean was "distributed" between several doctors — a tibia here; a cranium there; an ulna someplace else — where he made a meaningful contribution to medical science ... and the betterment of mankind...finally.

THE EXECUTION OF
JACK LAMBERT

In the summer of 1886, a young school teacher named Robert L. Madison visited the town of Charleston, now Bryson City, in Swain County, N. C. to discuss the possibility of establishing a school system somewhere in the area. On arriving in the village, Madison found more than two-thousand people crowding the streets. Inquiring as to the reason, Madison learned that there was to be a public execution and a gallows had been constructed in the center of the village near the present site of the First Baptist Church. Madison immediately announced his desire to leave, but his friends persuaded him to stay. As a consequence, the young man witnessed the last *legal* hanging in western North Carolina.

The man scheduled for execution was a Cherokee named Andrew Jackson (Jack) Lambert, who allegedly had shot and killed Dick Wilson, a Confederate hero and the Superintendent of Education in neighboring Jackson County. Owing to the popularity of Wilson and the anger of the citizenry of Jackson County, Lambert had been transferred to the Asheville jail until time for the execution. However, Madison quickly discovered that a considerable number of people living in Charleston and the Qualla community on the Cherokee Reservation had doubts as to Lambert's guilt. Madison learned that the shooting had occurred at night in the Savannah section of Jackson County; there were no witnesses to the murder, and the evidence which had convicted Lambert was circumstantial. Witnesses could only note that they

57

had seen two men struggling in the dark. The pistol found by Wilson's body was a five-shot, .32-caliber, "owl's head" revolver, a distinctive weapon, and one known to be owned by Jack Lambert.

Madison talked to several friends of Lambert who told the young teacher that Lambert not only maintained his innocence, but had told several people, "I didn't shoot Dick Wilson, but my gun did." Lambert's friends felt that the Cherokee's gun had been stolen and used by someone else to murder Wilson; further, they felt Lambert knew who the real murderer was. As time for the hanging approached, a small group of armed men surrounded the scaffold and waited for Sheriff Rich of Buncombe County to arrive with the prisoner. Sheriff Welch of Swain County would then bring Lambert to the gallows. Intrigued by the armed men, Madison asked questions and learned that a rumor had been circulating all morning about a planned rescue by friends of Lambert. This rumor and the mixed feeling of the audience created an atmosphere of considerable tension. The armed men stood within a roped off area facing the festive crowd, nervously awaiting Lambert's arrival.

Moments before the execution, a large group of Cherokees, including the wife and family of the condemned man, arrived in a wagon drawn by two horses. The crowd made way for the family, which took up a position immediately before the gallows. Sheriff Welch brought Lambert to the scaffold and prepared him for execution. The Cherokee's arms and legs were restrained by ropes and a black cap was placed over his head. Then, as though by some pre-arranged agreement with the condemned man, Sheriff Rich made his way through the crowd. Standing on the ground facing Lambert, Rich suddenly spoke in a loud, clear voice:

"Jackson Lambert, in the presence of Almighty God, of eternity, and of this great throng of people, I ask you, did you kill Dick Wilson?" Without hesitation, and in a voice filled with conviction, Lambert answered, "I did not." In the ensuing silence, Sheriff Welch stepped forward and grasped Lambert's piniioned hand, attempting an awkward handshake. Since his official duties included that of executioner, he walked quickly across the scaffold and down the steps where he "sprang the trap."

As Lambert dropped, a groan swept through the crowd. Madison heard a woman scream, someone fainted and scores of spectators turned their eyes away. As Lambert hung between heaven and earth, Madison turned to look at the faces of the dying man's family. Lambert's wife, Lucy Ann, was especially noteworthy. Unblinking, her face rigid and pale, she stoically watched her husband die. A fellow teacher from Ohio fell at Madison's feet, and Madison turned to see others who had fallen or were being assisted away by friends. Then an attending physician announced that the fall had not broken the victim's neck. Consequently, the silent crowd stood and watched Lambert slowly suffocate.

It took fourteen minutes. In the dreadful silence, the dying man's breathing was clearly audible. Madison and a mute audience watched Lambert's shoulders rise and fall, each convulsion weaker then the last. Stunned, the young teacher yearned for escape. He, the spectators and Lambert seemed trapped in a frozen moment, like figures in a painting.

The silence was broken by the doctor's pronouncement, "This man is dead." Then the frozen scene exploded with movement. Lambert's body was taken down, and the family immediately moved forward with a rude coffin. Placing the lifeless body in it, they raced to the waiting wagon. Madison noted that the Cherokees left in great haste; however, his attention was drawn to a small group of impatient spectators who gathered around the scaffold where they watched Sheriff Welch untie the hangman's noose. Using his pocket knife, Welch cut the white rope into short sections and threw them to the waiting spectators. The pieces of rope would be valued, not only as souvenirs, but as charms to ward off sickness and bad luck.

Later, Madison learned that a few miles away on the lonely mountain road to Qualla, near a place called "Scary Branch," a doctor waited. There, Lambert's family and friends dragged the corpse from the wagon and attempted to revive him. With the aid of a galvanic battery, the doctor vainly attempted to stimulate the dead man's heart. By kneading the lifeless flesh and pressing on the dead man's chest, the entire family strove to bring Jackson Lambert back to life.

This then, was the rumored rescue: not an armed band that swept down with whoops and gunfire to rescue their friend from the scaffold, but companions and relatives who waited by the gallows with a horse-drawn wagon and a coffin ... hoping, despite the doctor's dread pronouncement that they could snatch this husband, brother and friend back from the grave.

In later years, Madison frequently told the story of Jackson Lambert. "This happened when I was a beardless youth," he would begin. In a series of articles entitled *Experiences of a Pedagogue in the Carolina Highlands*, Madison recounted tales of earthquakes, railroad disasters and heroism. There was much to tell, for Robert Lee Madison had been privileged to be present on momentous occasions. He had gone on to be the founder of Western Carolina University and became something of a living legend in the little village of Webster where he frequently sat on summer evenings with his wife playing Bach and Schubert on a flute (his wife on the guitar).

Half a century after Jack Lambert's execution, Madison heard that a man on his deathbed in Dillsboro had told his family that he wished to confess to a crime that had haunted him all of his life. "I killed Dick Wilson," he said. "Jack Lambert was innocent." (See Postscript) And then, Madison would recount that day; describe again the woman's face who watched her husband die, and that last frantic dash with Jack Lambert's corpse down the Qualla Road. "So many stories," Madison would say, "So many sad, wonderful, tragic stories! Have I told you about the night they buried Traveler? No? Well, I grew up in the home of Robert E. Lee! Yes! And when I was about six...."

But that is another story.

G.C.

It is now a matter of record that the day prior to his execution, Jack Lambert wrote a twenty-page letter to his brothers in which he vowed his innocence. He described how he had been robbed of his money and his gun as he slept in a wagon near Savannah community. He further stated that he had kept silent because he had been assured that if he identified the actual killer, there would be immediate reprisals against his family. Some *eighty* years later, the family of Jack Lambert revealed this letter to the descendants of Dick Wilson. The children of the murdered man were long dead.

It is also a matter of record that some thirty years prior to the revelations involving Lambert's letter, a man named Will Jones called Sheriff Mason of Jackson County to his death bed and signed a full confession. He stated that the shooting was more an accident than a premeditated murder, and that he had used Jack Lambert's pistol. He did not reveal the names of those who conspired with him to supress the actual facts, though.

FRANKIE SILVER

Great God! How shall I be forgiven?
Not fit for earth, not fit for Heaven,
But little time to pray to God,
For now I try that awful road.

— Ballad of Frankie Silver

It was a bitter, cold day in late December, 1831, when John Silver found his way to the isolated Tennessee farm, forty miles from his own home in Burke County, N.C. Shivering in the brisk wind, with snow swirling, he climbed the steps and knocked. Momentarily, the door opened slightly, and an elderly man peered out.

"Are you Mr. Williams?" asked Silver. The man nodded but made no move to open the door further.

"My name is John Silver." He hesitated a moment and added, "I came about your slave ... the one that conjures. I been told how he can find missing folks." Williams opened the door.

"Jonas ain't here. Let him leave for Christmas so he could visit his family on a farm over the mountain 'n he won't be back till the second week of January." Williams paused before asking, "What's your trouble?"

"My boy Charlie disappeared a week ago." Silver shuffled his feet. "I got a feeling that something bad happened to him."

Williams ushered Silver into the house. While John warmed before a roaring fire, the farmer disappeared into the adjoining room. Within minutes he was back with a small glass globe attached to a long string.

"This is Jonas' conjurin' plumb-bob. He says that anybody can make it work, 'n I've seen him use it. Me 'n Jonas found a man last fall that drowned." Climbing into a chair, Williams tied the string to a rafter.

"You will have to make me a map."

"Beg pardon?" Puzzled, Silver watched Williams clamber down. "Map?"

Williams took a wrinkled piece of foolscap and a pencil stub from a shelf and handed them to Silver. "Draw all the places where your son might be. Put his house in the center. Then put down the creeks he crosses 'n any trails that he walks when he leaves home."

Beginning with a crude square representing the cabin where Charlie lived with his wife, Silver awkwardly scrawled lines and patterns: the Toe River, Deyton's Bend and the encircling mountains. Seating himself, Williams placed the map on the floor. Then he drew back the globe and released it.

"Now you 'n me, we set and stare at the plumb-bob 'n think 'bout your boy."

The globe swung in a great arc over Silver's drawing. Silver fixed his eyes on it while he thought of his son's face and his hearty laugh. Gradually the pendulum swings diminished until movement was barely perceptible. Then the globe stopped. Revolving at the end of the string, the glass pendant hung straight down.

"Now that's strange," said Williams. "I never seen it do that before."

Silver, who had feared his son's corpse was in the ice-bound Toe River or lying frozen on a mountain trail, thought the conjuring had failed. Disappointed, he stared for a moment at the arrested globe before slowly rising to leave.

"I guess it didn't work this time," he said. "Maybe you have to have Jonas to make it work."

"Ah, but I think it worked," said Williams. Gingerly he prodded the string, but the globe held its position like the needle of a compass, directly over the crude square on the map that represented the cabin of Charlie and Frankie Silver.

"I think you had it right when you said something bad has happened to your boy ... but it happened to him at home."

John Silver stared at the motionless globe. Then, suddenly, understanding dawned on his face.

While John Silver was descending a frozen mountain trail in Tennessee, his neighbors were searching the river banks and coves of Burke County. According to Charlie's wife, Frankie, her husband had left a few days before Christmas after spending the previous day cutting firewood. "He wanted to go hunting," she explained, "so he cut and racked a week's supply before leaving."

It was the firewood that first aroused the suspicions of Jake Cullis.

A quiet, elderly man and close friend of the Silver family, Cullis watched the fruitless search with growing alarm. When he heard Frankie talking about the firewood, he saw no reason to doubt her. In fact, he had passed the Silver cabin while Charlie was splitting chunks of hickory and stacking them on the porch. What bothered Cullis was the fact that the wood was gone. True, the nights were cold, but a week's supply of heat burned in a single night? Something was amiss.

As the search dragged on, Cullis found himself drawn to the cabin, now deserted since Frankie had taken baby Nancy and gone to stay with her parents.

"I'm not staying alone in a cabin with a baby and no firewood," she told the neighbors. "As for Charlie, since he didn't even bother to come home for Christmas, I don't care if he comes home or not."

Cullis noted that at no time did the young wife seem concerned about what might have happened to her husband. There was something else, too. Frankie had asked her in-laws to feed the cow while she and Nancy were away, adding that Charlie had fed her the morning before he left. Yet when

Alfred Silver, Charlie's seventeen-year-old brother, had gone to attend to the chores, he reported that the only footprints around the cow's stall were made by a woman's shoes.

The day following her departure, Frankie returned to the cabin for clothes. She found Jake Cullis standing in the yard. "I'd like to come inside for a minute, Frankie," he said. When she opened the door, Cullis went directly to the fireplace where he found a huge mound of ashes. Taking a long, wooden staff, Cullis stirred the cold heap, noticing that there was a plentiful supply of small objects — stone, bits of metal and bone.

While Frankie watched him nervously, he removed a small, blackened object and carried it to the kitchen. Filling a glass from the water bucket, he dropped the object in. There was a swirl of bubbles. Fixing Frankie with an accusing eye, Jake Cullis said, "Grease bubbles, Frankie. Them ashes is full of grease."

Seizing his staff, Cullis abruptly left the cabin. Following him to the doorway, Frankie was startled to see a large number of neighbors standing in her yard. Apparently Cullis had shared his suspicions with others. Moving about the yard, Cullis prodded the ground with his staff. Near the spring, he found a recently dug hole, packed with ashes. Churning the clotted debris with his staff, the old man removed a blackened oblong of metal. As he inspected it, a gasp came from one of Frankie's neighbors.

"I recognize that," he said. "That's a buckle from one of Charlie's hunting boots." All eyes moved from the object in Cullis' hand to Frankie Silver's face. She stood pale and trembling in the doorway. As the crowd moved towards the cabin, Frankie stood silently alone.

Within moments, the neighbors had found an array of grisly items. There were teeth and bone fragments in the fireplace; the mantel and floor were scored with hack marks; Cullis found an axe with a badly nicked blade. "Looks like this axe has been chopping something besides firewood," he said. Then, turning to the flooring, Jake pointed. "Look at them planks."

Charlie Silver's mother moved to the front of the group. "Frankie told me that she scoured the whole cabin after Charlie went hunting." The group stared at the spotless floor. Cullis said, "Let's pry up a couple of boards." Within moments the planks were removed and inspected. The underside of each plank was stained with blood, and the earth beneath the cabin was dark with gore. Throughout the search, Frankie stood, pale and trembling, in the crowd's midst.

The most grisly evidence was yet to come. A hollow tree stump a short distance from the cabin was found to contain a collection of "unburnable" items, including intestines, a liver and a heart.

Realizing that emotions were beginning to run high, one of the neighbors had the presence of mind to send for the Burke County Sheriff. When W.C. Butler arrived, he found the Silver cabin packed with angry people.

It was immediately apparent that the group was divided into opposing camps. Frankie stood with her eyes downcast as the storm of charges and counter charges raged between the Silver and Stewart relatives. After getting some semblance of order, Butler spoke to Frankie.

"Frankie, are you guilty of this terrible thing?" Frankie shook her head from side to side.

"She's guilty as sin," said Jake Cullis. "She murdered poor Charlie, cut him up and burned him!"

Looking around the room, Butler noted that many of Charlie Silver's immediate family were present. Butler proceeded with caution.

"One thing that bothers me about this," said the sheriff. "Look at Frankie. Are you folks telling me that she killed a man who was more than twice her weight and maybe three times as strong? Then, that little woman wrestled a corpse around all night, chopped it to pieces and burned it?" Someone said, "Maybe she had help."

Butler considered the possibility. "Maybe she did."

Charlie Silver's mother, her face haunted by the grim discoveries she had witnessed in the last few hours, spoke. "I can tell you this, Sheriff. Barbara Stewart and her son, Blackston, made no secret of the fact that they hated my boy."

"What about Isaiah, Frankie's father?" asked Butler.

"He's been away from home for weeks," said Cullis.

Within hours, Butler had arrested Frankie's mother and brother, charging them as accomplices in Charlie's murder. The mother and son, along with Frankie, were taken to the Morganton jail on January 9, 1832.

Isaiah Stewart returned home to find part of his family in jail. He quickly acquired legal advice, and by January 17, Barbara and Blackston were released on bail. Frankie remained in jail.

On March 17, a grand jury reviewed the case and dropped all charges against the mother and brother. A "true bill" was returned against Frankie, and her trial was scheduled for March 29.

It is not surprising that the most damaging testimony against Frankie came from old Jake Cullis. In addition, the exhibit table in the courtroom contained an assortment of disturbing objects: teeth, bone fragments, Charlie's boot buckle and the axe with the badly nicked blade.

In spite of the overwhelming circumstantial evidence, the jury did not readily convict Frankie. They repeatedly requested permission to talk further with witnesses and reluctantly discarded the possibility of accomplices. But in the end, the expected verdict came: Frances Silver was sentenced to be "hung by the neck until dead," thus becoming the first woman to receive the death sentence in the state of North Carolina.

There were a number of legal delays and postponements. An appeal to the state supreme court failed, but the state's overburdened docket required several reschedulings of the execution date.

Finally, court was adjourned until the spring of 1833, thereby granting Frankie a six-month reprieve. This delay also gave the Stewart family the opportunity to plan and carry out Frankie's rescue from the Morganton jail.

One of Frankie's brothers had a remarkable talent for woodcarving. For several weeks, each time he visited his sister's cell, he took the opportunity to study the lock. Subsequently, he carved a wooden key, which after testing it on the cell lock himself, he passed to Frankie.

The following night, Frankie unlocked her cell and fled to a nearby alley where an uncle waited with a hay-filled wagon. The uncle cut Frankie's long, blonde hair and gave her men's clothing. Concealed under the hay, Frankie put on pants, a shirt and a hat. When dawn broke in Morganton, the wagon rolled out of town with Frankie walking behind. Anyone witnessing the departure would assume that the figure strolling in the wagon's wake was a farm boy returning home after a night in town.

When Frankie's escape was discovered, a posse was immediately dispatched with orders to stop and question all travelers on the road. When Frankie saw the posse approaching, she decided to brazen it out. The leader of the posse halted his horse near Frankie and studied the small figure, finally leaning towards her and saying, "Frances Silver?"

Frankie peered at him from beneath her over-sized hat and replied in a deep baritone, "My name is Tommy."

"Yes," said the nervous uncle, from up on the wagon seat. "Her name is Tommy."

Back in the Morganton jail, Frankie was more closely watched. At the spring court, the date for the hanging was set for June 28 and postponed until July 12. It was during the last few weeks, when one of Frankie's close friends visited her, that Frankie allegedly confessed. According to the story, Frankie asked her confidante not to reveal the admission until after her death.

According to the close friend, the motive was jealousy. Frankie said that her husband's numerous "hunting trips" were really cover-ups for involvement with women, married and single. Frankie confronted Charlie with what she had learned about his drinking and dancing with other women, but the erring husband had merely laughed at her. Frankie had vowed not to be further humiliated by her husband's unfaithfulness.

On the fatal day when Charlie split and stacked a week's supply of firewood, Frankie decided that he intended to be gone for a week, leaving his wife and baby to spend Christmas alone. When Charlie, exhausted from his labor, entered the house, he picked up the baby Nancy and stretched out on a sheepskin rug before the fireplace. When he dozed off, Frankie removed Nancy from Charlie's arms, placed her on the bed and retrieved the axe from the porch.

She struck Charlie with all the strength she had, hoping to kill him with a single blow. Instead, the stricken man struggled to his feet, clutching the deep wound in his neck. As Charlie staggered about the room, a gyser of blood splashed the walls and floor. Frankie buried herself under the bed quilts, covering her ears to drown out Charlie's moans. When he finally collapsed on the floor, she found the axe and struck him again. The second blow was fatal.

As she lay in bed watching firelight flicker on the walls and ceiling of the little cabin, with Charlie's body on the floor, she hatched the scheme of destroying all the evidence of her crime. It was a labor that took the better part of the night and most of the newly-cut firewood. At times, the fire's heat was so intense Frankie found it difficult to remain in the cabin.

Near daylight, Frankie discovered that although Charlie's body was gone, the walls and floor were coated with blood, grease and axe slashes. With the remaining wood, she boiled water to wash and scrub every tell-tale sign away.

In addition to her alleged confession, there is a lugubrious poem that Frankie supposedly wrote during her final days and read from the scaffold. It is a straight-forward confession, admitting premeditation. Part of one stanza states, *For days and months, I spent my time/Thinking of how to commit this crime.* The poem has been set to music and is frequently published in accounts of Frankie's execution. There is reason, however, to believe that the "poetic confession" was composed by a hand other than Frankie's.

Some say Frankie never confessed. In addition, there are accounts that attribute other sins to Charlie Silver. Drinking and wife beating, for instance. According to this version, Charlie had been warned repeatedly by Isaiah Stewart that if he continued to misuse Frankie, he would be held accountable.

There is one final, memorable and provocative image of Frankie Silver. According to eyewitness accounts, on the day she climbed the gallows steps, someone handed her a piece of cake. As she stood there facing the crowd that had come to watch her die, the executioner asked if she had anything to say before he placed the noose around her neck.

Frankie's face brightened and she moved to the front of the scaffold as though preparing to speak. Isaiah Stewart's voice boomed from the crowd, "Die with it in ye, Frankie!"

Frankie nodded and stepped back, positioning herself over the trap door.

"Are you ready, Frankie?" asked the hangman.

"Let me finish my cake," replied Frankie. She ate the last bite, dusted the crumbs from her hands, reached for the black hood the hangman held in his hand and pulled it over her head, blotting out the world forever.

G.C.

PART III

REMARKABLE PEOPLE
(AND A BEAR)

IONA'S SON

On February 6, 1863, a clear, cold morning in Clay County, North Carolina, George Marstellar saddled his horse to ride the four miles between his farm and that of his friend, Robert Henry. George knew something was wrong. For several years now, he and Robert had "shared" slaves. The system had turned out to be mutually beneficial with the two farmers dividing all attending expenses. The slaves became accustomed to working at the two farms on alternate days. However, on the previous evening, Mostellar received a message from Henry stating he had a situation that needed immediate attention. Could he retain the slaves for part of the following day?

George was curious. Such a request had never come before, and his long acquaintance with the ninety- eight year old Henry told him that the problem was something other than a broken fence or a leaking roof. However, on arriving at Henry's farm, George was warmly greeted by the genial old man. Marstellar accepted an invitation to dinner, and his previous misgivings vanished as he watched Henry eat with relish. Marstellar had always admired the elder man's intelligence and had spent many evenings listening to him discuss philosophy, theology and literature. This day was no exception.

"By the way, the cook fixed your favorite, rhubarb pie, and I've opened a bottle of that claret you're so fond of."

"So," thought George, "he knew I was coming." This wasn't the first time he had arrived at Henry's house to find a second plate at the table and his favorite wine already poured. Lifting his glass, George noted that the meal was no hurried repast. Indeed, the variety of food suggested that this was a special occasion.

Finally, Marstellar ventured to inquire about Henry's message on the previous day.

"Oh, that!" said Henry, pouring himself another glass of wine. "They should be finished by now. They are digging a grave for me."

"So Julius has finally died," said Marstellar, thinking of Henry's ancient mule.

"Ah, no," said Henry, rising to toast his friend. "Julius is fine." As their glasses clinked, Marstellar noticed the familiar twinkle in Henry's eyes. Henry drank his wine and then smiling, said, "The grave is for me."

Instantly, the younger man knew Henry was sincere, yet he perceived no indication of anxiety or gloom in his friend's behavior. Henry began to talk enthusiastically about the Greek philosophers, and within moments he was discoursing on Heraclitus. The two men moved to the parlor as Henry continued talking. Shortly, Marstellar saw the old man's eyes move to the clock, and then without further ado, he arranged a bearskin in front of the fireplace and laid down on it. Within moments, he was dead. In later years, as Marstellar related this remarkable incident, he said the old man died as though he were keeping a long-standing appointment.

Robert Henry's death is no less remarkable than his life. Indeed, the early history of Southern Appalachia affords few examples of individuals with such varied talents. There is considerable confusion about Henry's origin and parentage. The most commonly accepted version states he was one of sixteen children born to an ex-British soldier, Thomas Henry and wife, Martha Shield Henry. At the time of his birth, his parents were attempting to travel from Virginia to Georgia. Finding themselves at the mercy of winter storms, the family took shelter in "a rail pen" constructed for cattle. There, on January 10, 1765, Robert Henry was born. Shortly afterwards, Thomas Henry gave up his plan of moving to Georgia and settled in Iredell County, N.C., later moving to Mecklenburg. Robert Henry told his grandchildren that at age ten, he traveled with his father to town where he witnessed the signing of the Mecklenburg Declaration. Henry said he did not understand the significance of the event for many years.

Lyman C. Draper, the author of *King's Mountain and Its Heroes*, mentions a sixteen-year-old soldier named Robert Henry who was bayoneted by a British soldier during an early engagement. Henry later wrote Draper that he inadvertently fired his rifle, killing the soldier when he was stabbed and found that his attacker's bayonet had pierced his hand, pinning it to his thigh. A friend of Henry's named William Caldwell attempted to help his injured friend by pulling the bayonet from his thigh. When he experienced difficulty in removing the weapon, Caldwell placed his heel on the injured limb and pulled the bayonet free. Henry afterwards noted that he experienced more pain from his friend's rescue than from the original injury! Draper goes on to acknowledge a deep debt to Henry for many of the details concerning the battle. Specifically, Henry wrote a detailed account of the action as he experienced it. Draper notes that Henry's writing proved invaluable since the young soldier had a remarkable talent for reconstructing the events of the battle.

Several years later, a young teacher named Robert Henry moved to Buncombe County, N.C., and opened the first school west of the Blue Ridge. The school, named Union Hill, became noted for its accomplished teacher. However, by 1799, Henry had resigned his position to become a surveyor, participating in the running and marking of the dividing line between North Carolina and Tennessee. Within a few years, though, Henry had entered yet another profession, the law. In January 1806 he was named solicitor of Buncombe County and quickly became the most distinguished practitioner of criminal justice in the region.

Within a decade, Henry changed professions again, emerging as the owner and operator of a public resort called Sulphur Springs, later called Deaver's Springs and Carrier Springs (See "The Curse on Deaver's Springs"). Little is known of him after this. The annals of Buncombe County reveal that he had two sons, both of whom shared their father's uncanny intellect and ability to master diverse skills. For example, according to Manley Wade

Wellman in *Dead and Gone,* Henry's son James, "born when his father was seventy-three" could read the classics in several languages by the age of ten, and at nineteen became the editor of *The Asheville Spectator* (following Zebulon Vance). James read law but gave up journalism and a legal career to join the First North Carolina Cavalry. Becoming a Colonel at the age of twenty-six, he returned to Asheville, became a solicitor, was elected judge at thirty and died at forty-eight. According to his obituary, the accomplishments of his short life were equal to "four centenarians."

One historian, commenting on Robert Henry's life, noted that he was "a hunter, pioneer, soldier, school teacher, surveyor, lawyer, farmer, manufacturer, physician, hotel keeper, landlord, historian, author, politician and frontiersman." During his career, he was "a subject of King George III, of North Carolina, of North Carolina under Congressional Management, of North Carolina under the Articles of Confederation, then under the United States Constitution, ... and died a citizen of the Confederate States of America." The noted historian, John P. Arthur, was his grandson.

In addition to all these accomplishments, there is another. All his life, Henry had periods of premonition. He *knew* the future. He had a sense of impending events. Many of his successful economic ventures seemed to have been based on an almost supernatural awareness of things to come. According to Henry's descendants, he announced the premature death of both his sons prior to the events. Family tradition says that Mary Tidwell, Henry's granddaughter, witnessed the prophecies.

What are we to make of men like Robert Henry? Perhaps the historian Foster Soundley made the most insightful comment when discussing the origin of the first settlers in southern Appalachia. In tracing the cultural roots of Robert Henry and a host of men noted for remarkable talents in this country's early history, Soundley noted that a significant number originated in the geographic area of Scotland and Ireland that is near the half-mythical isle of Iona, an intellectual center since the time of the Druids. Here, according to legend, men's minds became aware "as though wakened from a dream." From this place scholars and saints went forth to teach. Here students as diverse as the legendary Merlin and the early Christian saints acquired a secret knowledge which was to be used to aid mankind in attaining its destiny. According to tradition, many of Iona's descendants passed along their knowledge to their children and to the children of others who were deemed worthy of receiving it. Many were noted for longevity. Could Robert Henry have been the bearer of such knowledge?

Since Robert Henry lived for nearly a century, he touched the lives of many people. Former students, grandchildren and associates remember one particular aspect of the man's life. Henry had no fear of death. He moved through life with a confidence that suggested he was fulfilling a preordained role. If we believe this, then there is no reason not to believe that on that cold winter afternoon Robert Henry wrapped his bearskin about him like "... one lies down to pleasant dreams" and closed his eyes as his astonished neighbor watched ... like a man who had accomplished his mission, and now must leave to keep his appointment of long-standing.

G.C.

NOTE: Although the majority of accounts treat Robert Henry's life with respect, readily acknowledging him to be one of North Carolina's most remarkable sons, there are two notable exceptions. Judge Robert Strange in his autobiographical novel, *Eoneguski*, published in 1839, provides an extremely unflattering description of Henry's physical appearance in the character of Mr. Johns. N.C. Browder in his *The Cherokee Indians and Those Who Came After* also provides an unflattering character sketch and goes so far as to suggest that many of the details of Henry's life are a self-created fiction. In essence, Browder finds it impossible to believe that any one human being could have accomplished so much or could have been present on so many fortuitous occasions.

View from the cemetery where Mark Cathey is buried. Overlooks the town of Bryson City, N.C., toward the Great Smoky Mountains.

CAUGHT BY
THE GOSPEL HOOK

Mark Cathey's sister was worried. "Out there traipsing around in the woods after the doctor told him he has a weak heart," she muttered. The old man had left that afternoon with his squirrel rifle and his dog, and here it was getting dark. Making up her mind, the sister contacted several of Mark's friends. "I'd appreciate it if you would check that little cove where he sometimes goes."

They found him beneath an old hickory looking like a man who had just sat down for a moment to enjoy the afternoon. His rifle lay across his lap, and the dog slept peacefully by his side. Mark Cathey was dead at seventy-three.

Born William Marcus Cathey in 1871, he had been one of eight children. During his remarkable life, he had been a hunter, fisherman, trapper and guide. Before his death in 1944, his reputation had spread far beyond his mountain home in Swain County, N.C. The rich and powerful found their ways to Mark's door to request his services as a guide for hunting and fishing parties.

Like many mountain men at the turn of the century, Mark had found his first employment with a lumber camp. Agile and athletic, he quickly became a log-roller, one of the most dangerous activities connected with transporting logs down mountain streams. Working with cant-hooks and hand-spikes, the rollers raced along the bank, frequently riding the logs down rapids. When jams occurred, it was the roller's job to break them up. River banks were often slippery and treacherous, and rollers ran the constant risk of being either crushed by ponderous logs or drowned in the mountain flumes.

When the logging camps closed down, leaving a score of deserted towns and thousands of acres of devastated forests throughout western North Carolina, Mark Cathey was out of work. But unlike many of his neighbors who moved north, Cathey returned to the forests. There were still tracts of wilderness around Hazel Creek and Deep Creek, secluded coves teeming with wildlife. It was to these places that Cathey gave his heart.

Within a short time, hunters around Bryson City and the Cherokee Indian Reservation began to talk about him. One of his hunting companions, S.J. Hunnicut, remembered, "I was supposed to be one of the best when it came to hunting and fishing, but I was always second to Mark." Cathey's knowledge was remarkable. "He knew *where* to go, *when* to go and *what* to take in terms of equipment."

"People used to come just to watch him fish," said Cathey's sister. "When they watched him catch a dozen brown trout before breakfast, they were convinced he knew something they didn't know. How else could you explain him catching fish from stretches of water where other fishermen had fished just minutes before?"

One of Cathey's friends remembered the contrast between Mark's equipment and that of the well-heeled Easterners who hired him as a guide. "Here these guys would stand in their fancy waders with expensive fishing rods and a tackle box with maybe two-hundred dry flies in it. And Mark, well, Mark wore overalls and he had this little lightweight rod made out of split bamboo. Usually his only fly was a gray hackle with a yellow body."

Yes, Mark Cathey knew something. Most of his friends commented on his fishing technique. "He had a way of moving that fly on water, what he called a 'skippity-hop' that none of us could quite imitate. Mark called it 'running 'em crazy.'"

"I camped with him once," said Hunnicut. "While I was gathering firewood, he said he thought he would catch a few trout for supper. After I'd gathered the wood and he hadn't come back to camp I decided to go find him and do a little fishing of my own. As I was fishing my way back towards camp, I come on Mark. He had ninety-nine trout. I apologized for interrupting him, and he said, 'Well, if you hadn't come along, I would have caught an even hundred.'"

Hunting was the same. Bear, deer or pheasant, Mark knew where they were. When the wealthy Easterners arrived, he would ask them what they wanted to hunt. Then he would set out with them to some place like Cade's Cove, Deep Creek or Lost Horse. "He liked to watch them," said his sister. "When he would roust a bear or flush a quail, he would just sit back and watch them banging away. Most often, they missed everything."

Hunnicut recalled one particular trip. "I remember once we had a deer hunting party, and there was just too many people. Mark told me that it was going to be a mess — disorganized and dangerous — so we agreed that we had to eliminate about half the group. What he done was, he set up 'stands.' He told the standers that all they had to do was wait for us to flush deer and drive them back. I took a group on a bogus nine mile drive through some of the roughest country I could find. Mark did the same. At the end of the day, half of the hunters had deserted. Then Mark announced, 'Well, now we have a hunting party of manageable size. Let's start.'"

As Cathey's fame grew, he found himself acting as a guide for Hollywood stars, writers and politicians. He was often offered employment in other places. He invariably declined saying he lived in the best place on earth. In 1938, a movie agent attempted to lure Mark to Hollywood. "All you have to do is drive a team of oxen in a movie," said the agent. "We will wine and dine you and pay you well." Despite such repeated offers, Cathey decided to stay at home.

Several weeks before his death, Cathey's sister scolded him. "Now you know what the doctor said, Mark. You can't go climbing up and down creeks and hollers with a bad heart."

The life-long bachelor smiled and replied, "Well, when my time comes, I'd rather it was out there in the woods than anywhere else." Then, taking his squirrel rifle and his dogs, he vanished down the trail.

83

Cathey's tombstone is on a high hill overlooking the town of Bryson City. Not far away is the grave of another famous woodsman, Horace Kephart, author of *Our Southern Highlanders*. Occasionally, people climb the hill to visit Cathey's grave, perhaps prompted by curiosity about the whimsical message on the stone:

MARK CATHEY
BELOVED HUNTER AND FISHERMAN
WAS HIMSELF CAUGHT BY THE GOSPEL HOOK
JUST BEFORE THE SEASON CLOSED FOR GOOD

N.A./G.C.

Mark Cathey's headstone

Cashiers, N.C. Whiteside Mountain, at 4,930 feet, overlooks
the Cashiers area, a valley 3,500 feet high in the
Blue Ridge Mountains.

FOOL'S ROCK

All Gus Baty ever wanted was for Irene Edwards to notice him. That was all.

In later years when he talked about that May morning in 1911, he spoke with wry humor of the extremes to which a young man would go to attract a woman's attention. From the time the little group of picnickers left Durgan Corner in Highlands (seven walking and six riding in a surrey) until they completed the six-mile trek to Whiteside Mountain, Gus used every trick he knew. Even the silver plate didn't work!

While working at Ducktown, Tennessee, Gus had suffered a head injury. The doctor felt that Baty's skull fracture needed additional protection, so he implanted a small silver plate. Gus soon discovered that he possessed an object that made him interesting — especially to girls. Gingerly, they would tap the small silver disc while Gus recounted his brush with death in Ducktown. Did it hurt? Could he feel the sun on it? They found him interesting. Well, all except Irene Edwards.

The group stopped to eat lunch before going on to Whiteside Mountain, and the twenty-three-year-old Baty was becoming more and more distressed. In addition to ignoring Gus's overtures, Irene was listening raptly to everything teenager Harvey McCall said. Baty not only found himself rejected but replaced by a younger man! As the two young people laughed and whispered, Baty became quiet and withdrawn, sipping from a pint of whiskey he carried in his pocket.

Leaving the surrey behind, the group's unofficial chaperones, Will Dillard and his wife Maude, Charlie Wright and his wife Helen, joined the young people as they walked to the mountain's crest. Noticing the despondent Baty, Wright suggested he leave the bottle behind in the surrey and join the crowd. Baty put the whiskey in his pocket instead and turned to join a group walking towards Fool's Rock.

In later years, members of the group always commented on the beauty of the view that day. Certainly most views are breath-taking on the top of Whiteside, but this spring day the visibility was perfect. The corridors of mountains stretched away into Georgia, South Carolina and Virginia, and the group stood in the brisk wind, watching eagles wheel and drop into their mountain aeries. It was then that Gus Baty made his final bid for Irene's attention.

Racing to Fool's Rock, Baty turned and announced to the group that he was going to jump. Leaping out onto Fool's Rock which projects from the side of the mountain, Baty pretended to teeter on the edge, wind-milling his arms as though struggling for balance. Baty's performance frightened the group and several people entreated him to return. Finally, two young men approached Baty, seized him by the arms and dragged him from his perch. Disengaging himself, Baty returned to his air-borne stage, stumbled and fell.

For a moment, the spectators were stunned. Where just a second ago Gus had danced, there was only the expanse of space and distant mountains. They heard only the sound of wind and the faint cry of eagles. Then pandemonium broke. "He's gone!" they screamed. "Help! Gus fell off the mountain!" Among those calling was Irene. At last, Gus had gotten her attention.

The two chaperone couples were a short distance away watching the eagles rise and fall in the rivers of wind surging around the mountain's top. Hearing the screams, Charlie Wright immediately hurried to the group which was now milling around in confusion. Understanding that Gus had fallen, Charlie stepped out on the rock, laid down and looked over the edge. Some sixty-five feet below lay Gus, his feet tangled in a rhododendron bush, dangling over almost two-thousand feet of empty space. Gus had only fallen about fifteen feet but had acquired a variety of sprains, bruises and fractures. Striking a slanting ledge, he had bounced and rolled until his progress was halted by the rhododendron bush. Stunned, possibly unconscious, Baty lay inches from certain death.

It was Charlie Wright who volunteered to rescue Baty. Asking Will Dillard to help him, Wright descended a safe slope of Whiteside until he was parallel with Baty. Then he inched forward until he was on the sheer rock face of Whiteside with no handholds except the minute pits and crevices in the surface of the rock. Charlie kept his shoes on, using the leather soles in the granite surface. Then Will Dillard found himself in a quandary. Literally hanging by his fingers, Dillard found he could not continue. He called to Charlie that he was going back and began inching his way to safety. Wright went on, and within moments, the effort exerted by his fingers gripping the rough stone produced painful bleeding. Moving in a near-perpendicular stance, it took Wright two hours to reach Baty.

Watching from above, Helen Wright became hysterical. Twice her piercing screams disconcerted her husband, causing him to falter. Although Helen would become more agitated, all attempts to lead the distraught wife from the scene failed.

Wright arrived at a point slightly above Baty. Lowering himself with painful slowness, he grasped Baty's coat and dragged him upwards until he could get his shoulder under Baty's limp body. Wright spoke to Gus, assuring him that "everything will be alright." In all likelihood, the injured man was not fully conscious, but he stirred and smiled at Wright's voice.

Forcing himself erect, Wright knew he could not complete the rescue without help. Prolonged tension in the muscles of his arms and legs produced involuntary trembling and spasms. He called to Will Dillard, telling him that he needed help. It is much to Dillard's credit that he came without hesitation, once more traversing the space he had traveled earlier. Once Dillard arrived, Wright moved the semi-conscious Baty forward until he was between the two rescuers.

There is good reason to believe that Wright would have fallen to his death if Will Dillard had not assisted him. Within moments after Dillard's arrival, Wright lost his footing and slid downward several feet. His slide was halted by Dillard's hold on his friend's body. The three men were now at a point where rescue from above was possible.

Tying together the lines and halters from Dillard's surrey, the men on the crest of the mountain lowered a lifeline. Once Baty was securely tied, he was pulled to safety. Three hours had lapsed since Gus Baty fell from Fool's Rock.

Six months after Gus Baty's fall, an article in the *Charlotte Observer* gave a detailed account of the rescue. The story prompted several of the state's influential people to recommend Charlie Wright for a Carnegie Award for Bravery. The letters resulted in the Carnegie Foundation sending a representative to Highlands. According to several eyewitnesses, the representative was taken to Whiteside Mountain and after a nervous peek at the location of the rescue, he immediately stated there was no question about Wright's and Dillard's courage. Wright received the first gold medal ever awarded by the Foundation and $2000 in cash; Will Dillard received a silver medal and $1000 in cash. (It is interesting to note that only nineteen gold Carnegie medals have ever been awarded.)

Both Wright and Dillard bought farms with their money. Ironically, Charlie Wright died on December 4, 1927, when his truck plunged over a rocky precipice near Lake Toxaway.

As for Gus Baty, he became a carpenter and house builder and lived to be eighty-two years old. Several of the houses he built can still be seen in the area. Most of his friends say he was a quiet man, and although he did not volunteer information about his fall, he would talk freely about it when asked. He always seemed a bit embarrassed when friends introduced him as "the man who fell off Whiteside Mountain."

As the years passed, Baty's fall began to undergo the inevitable transition from fact to myth. Old-timers in Highlands still will tell you about the Carnegie representative who did not feel that Wright's act deserved a medal — until Charlie's friends seized the man and lowered him in a makeshift harness from Fool's Rock for "a better look." According to myth, the representative fainted.

In 1952, *The State* magazine published an account of the rescue that was filled with "local color" myths and distortions, including some highly imaginative dialogue between Baty and Wright during the rescue. There was also an account of Gus's bottle of whiskey which, according to the magazine, was still in the rhododendron bush where Charlie Wright placed it after removing it from Baty's pants pocket in 1911. Occasionally the more gullible will peer vainly over the edge of the mountain, hoping to catch a glimpse of that pint bottle.

Gus frequently acknowledged that he "got a little tired" of telling people there was no bottle down there. According to Gus, the bottle broke when he fell, and his friends and relatives noted that after his rescue Gus Baty never drank again.

According to Bill Marett, author of *Courage at Fool's Rock*, Irene Edwards married Charles Renault, who was a patient in the Tuberculosis Sanatorium on Bug Hill. They later moved to Ohio.

G.C.

Samantha Bumgarner

QUEEN OF
THE BANJO PICKERS

"Who's that?" asked the child, pointing to a woman sitting on a suitcase with musical instrument cases at her feet.

The grandfather took a look and replied, "Oh, that's Aunt Samantha. She's waiting for the bus, I reckon. Must be heading for a fiddling convention or something."

In Jackson County, N.C., Samantha Biddix Bumgarner was "Aunt Samantha," even to grandfathers who were certainly her elders. She received the honorary "Aunt" title not because of her age — she was in her thirties when the title stuck — but because her neighbors found a way to acknowledge all she had done.

Outside the mountain circle of friends, Samantha Bumgarner was "The Fiddling Ballad Woman of the Hills" or "Queen of the Banjo Pickers." One of the first females to make records of traditional mountain ballads, Aunt Samantha taught the world to enjoy tunes so old their origins were somewhere in Scotland or England.

Among those who had known her longest, Aunt Samantha's natural musical gifts were overshadowed by two other traits — an unusual style of playing and her unhesitating willingness to teach and encourage others. Her banjo technique was neither a clawhammer nor a bluegrass style. She moved downward with her index finger and back up with the forefinger, an easy technique for her, strange for others.

Her fame became widespread, and her life is the story of a mountain woman born "with music in her," who became a talented performer and a genuine folk musician, never passing up a chance to play or sing.

Born in 1878, Samantha grew up in a house full of music because her father, Has Biddix, was a fiddler. Has gave his daughter a banjo and taught her to play it. In short order, Samantha played well enough to perform with Has and his friends. Secretly Samantha longed to play the fiddle, too, but Has would not allow her to touch the instrument. As an adult, Samantha confessed to defying her father's ultimatum and sneaking around to practice the fiddle whenever he was gone.

By the time she reached womanhood, Samantha had mastered several instruments, including the banjo, cello, organ, mandolin, guitar and the fiddle. But she did not own her own violin until she married Carse Bumgarner, and he gave her one. After the young couple's house burned and Samantha's banjo was lost, it was replaced with what Samantha called "a ten cent banjo," but even with a cheap instrument and a serious attack of nervousness, she made one of her earliest marks of distinction by winning a fiddlers' convention at Canton, N.C.

She would win scores of other contests, and she would acquire a banjo to match her ability. In 1924, Columbia Records found her performing with Eva Smathers Davis. The two women accepted the record company's offer to record "Big-Eyed Rabbit" and "Wild Bill Jones." The records were so successful the women were called back to New York to eventually cut fourteen sides, including tunes such as "Fly Around Pretty Little Miss," "Worried Blues" and "Georgia Blues."

The two were special guest performers at the Atlanta Fiddlers' Convention, and a news article at the time reported that "the newly released records by the musical discoveries from North Carolina, now recording exclusively for the Columbia New Process Records are providing excellent sellers... [Bumgarner and Davis] sing and accompany themselves on banjo and violin. Their specialty is singing and playing real traditional American music, songs that are a part of our national lore."

When Robert Winslow Gordon came into the mountains to collect traditional ballads, he went first to see the legendary balladeer Bascom Lamar Lunsford. Lunsford then escorted Gordon to Samantha's house where recordings were made of Samantha playing and singing right in her home.

Three years later, after Lunsford decided to start a festival devoted to mountain music, he again made the long trip to Samantha's to ask if she'd be part of the festival. "It'll be real, honest music," he said. "The old tunes — and old-timey dancing." Naturally Samantha accepted, and the Mountain Dance and Folk Festival at Asheville, N.C. became one of the events she never missed.

As famous as she was, when Samantha heard that some Dillsboro neighbors, Joe and Annie Cagle, were musicians prone to move all the furniture out of the front room and play all night for as long as friends cared to dance, she went calling. At the Cagles, she found nine-year-old Harry Cagle struggling to imitate one of his mother's banjo licks.

"That young 'un just might make a banjo player," she said. "Let me take him and put it to him."

The adults laughed, but Harry hoped the neighbor was serious. The next day he appeared at Samantha's door, and she started his lessons. Harry was a quick study, and soon Samantha invited him to play with her at weekend performances. Making music with Samantha was where young Harry spent every free minute. In fact, the two were picking tunes under the trees in Samantha's backyard the day the big, shiny car with hub caps bearing the letter "B" pulled up.

"How are you?" asked Samantha. "How was your trip?"

"Fine. Just fine," replied Dr. John Brinkley, a physician famous across the United States for his goat gland operations. (See "Goat Gland King")

"You going to take that little dude with you?" Brinkley asked, nodding toward Harry.

"If he'll go I'll be glad to have him."

"I would, too," said Brinkley.

95

The deal obviously discussed earlier was sealed, and it included Harry. Within a few months Samantha, Harry and other members of Samantha's band headed to Mexico where Dr. Brinkley had established a radio station, XERA, just outside U.S. territory and therefore not subject to American broadcasting regulations. XERA's powerful signal was heard all across the continent. Even Harry's family back in the mountains could listen as Samantha and her band performed live from Mexico four times a day.

For more than a year, Samantha sang old-timey ballads from Mexico. The exposure meant most Americans heard her name and her music. When the troupe returned to the mountains, in part because of increasing U.S. pressure to shut down XERA, Samantha was just beginning to feel twinges of arthritis in her hands and shoulders.

She slowed down a bit but not much. She had always written songs, and now that she was well-known enough, she could perform and record her own tunes. She made more recordings, playing "Last Gold Dollar," a song she wrote about the time "the government took up all the gold."

The records sold well, and Samantha accepted offers to perform in New York, Washington, New Orleans, St. Louis, Chicago and Kansas City, but during August, she was always back in the mountains for Lunsford's Mountain Dance and Folk Festival. She became a perennial favorite at the festival. Her constant smile and quick moving hands seemed to become even livelier as she stood on stage, joking with the audience and urging them to join in. "You know, I had rather make music than to eat when I'm hungry," she said, and it was a statement audiences knew to be true.

By the 1950s interest in American ballads was apparent overseas, and Samantha traveled to Liverpool, England, to record some of her songs. So full of tunes was she that without bragging she once said, "I reckon I could play from now on and never play the same tune twice."

Europeans loved Aunt Samantha's music and her slightly larger than normal banjo decorated with a butterfly. A living legacy of American folk music, the cheerful and ready performer was quite popular, but in August she headed for the Mountain Dance and Folk Festival, a place where she always found kindred spirits ready to make music.

Each year at the festival young and old musicians sought her out. Never was she too busy to demonstrate or help in some way. It was during one of these festivals that the famous folk singer Pete Seeger approached her to ask about playing the banjo. Seeger's time with Samantha resulted in *How to Play the Banjo*, a book used by thousands of banjo students.

In 1955, *Life* magazine featured Samantha in an article about famous banjo players, and towards the end of her life she was described as "about the most complete music maker that ever came along." Despite all the praise, Aunt Samantha was never too famous to pick a few tunes with neighbors or play at hometown gatherings. Nothing in her life was more urgent than making music.

As she approached eighty, arthritis gnarled her fingers and a broken hip slowed her movements, but neither erased her smile or the music of her spirit. Even when she died on Christmas Eve, 1960, the music did not falter because Aunt Samantha Bumgarner had spent a lifetime passing along the rhythms and the melodies to all who love mountain music.

N.A.

Dr. John Romulus Brinkley

Cartoon from
The Kansas City Star

AMERICAN
GOAT GLAND KING

John Romulus Brinkley's life was made for a writer — it was a classic poor-boy-makes-good American tale. Out of orphaned poverty he became a man thousands of poor mountain children with dreams believed in. Before he died, Brinkley challenged several major governmental and social organizations and scared both the Democratic and Republican national parties. He was a hero to many Americans of less than high social birth because they saw him as one of them — an honest, capable, hardworking outsider from humble beginnings who succeeded because of native intelligence, resourcefulness and determination.

In fact, he repeatedly mentioned his roots — sometimes as a source of pride, an excuse for ignorance or naiveté, as an advertising gimmick or as an explanation for his conduct. While thousands of rural Americans saw John R. Brinkley as a persecuted, forward-thinking, anti-establishment leader, others saw him as a charlatan, a con man, a quack. Whatever the label, Brinkley was undeniably one mountain boy who left his mark on American life.

Born at a small North Carolina place called Beta, in Jackson County, known primarily as a cattle loading stop along the railroad line, John Romulus Brinkley was his young mother's only child. He was told early on that his second name was the name of an orphaned baby who grew up to build Rome. He must remember he was named for a builder, a creator, a man of lasting importance. He remembered.

By the time he was five, his mother was dead. When he was ten, his physician father died while with a patient. There had not been an excess of anything for young Brinkley up to this point, and with his father's death there was even less. He was an orphan in poverty, being raised by the only remaining relative he had, a maiden aunt of his mother's named Sally.

Obviously intelligent, John endured the scorn of better-off children who ridiculed his patched pants and bare feet because he knew school was necessary. He meant to be a physician, an important man called by God to help others. He intended to take his place among the greats -- that was where he knew he was meant to be. His own father had said that preachers and doctors were not made but called by God. He remembered that, too.

Although he knew he had a calling, poverty and no access to medical training stood in his way. Scores of mountain orphans just like him were being raised without enough food, heat or money, but Brinkley was different. He was driven, so he looked for ways to make money. He became a mail carrier. In the time he waited each day for the mail to arrive, he hung out at the Western Union office and learned Morse Code. The man at the railroad station always said young Brinkley was a "smart 'un."

He was hired as a telegraph operator and saved enough money to ride the train to the only large town he had heard much about, Asheville, N.C. There he saw electric lights, rode a street car, spent the night in a boarding house, used an indoor toilet, watched and listened to people he considered sophisticated -- and ate bananas. The trip changed his life; he now realized the world outside the mountains was accessible and full of opportunities.

Using the travel privileges associated with working for the railroad, Brinkley saw more of the world. As he aged, he moved from town to town, working for the railroad. When Aunt Sally, the woman who raised him, died in 1906, he returned to the mountains and was surprised when one of the girls who had tormented him earlier, a girl he considered "unattainable," flirted with him.

The two married and moved to Chicago where John entered Bennett Medical College, an eclectic school of medicine, which was not recognized by the allopathic medical circle and the ruling American Medical Association. Brinkley said later that as a poor boy straight from the country, he never thought to ask about the politics of the medical school; he simply wanted to be a physician.

He worked eight hours a day at Western Union and then attended medical classes while his marriage eroded. Nine months after the marriage, a daughter was born. Money was in short supply, but Brinkley doggedly kept up the schedule of work and study. In 1910, when classes were dismissed he requested double shifts at Western Union in order to pay off the mounting debts. He brought home his first double paycheck, and the next day both wife and child were gone.

The following period of Brinkley's life was consumed with finding his wife and child, nasty court wrangling and Brinkley kidnapping his daughter and going to Canada. Eventually the couple reconciled for a few months during which time Brinkley practiced medicine in the mountains of home. Physicians who could not pass the state licensing exam or who had not completed the required training were allowed to practice in areas where there was a shortage of doctors, and western North Carolina was one of those places.

Brinkley's resourcefulness, a trait that would show itself throughout his life, served the new country doctor well. Working with a set of medical instruments he purchased from a pawn shop, Brinkley learned to use whatever was at hand. When he was called to see an elderly man choking on meat skin, he did not have the necessary tools to treat the man conventionally. He looked around the yard -- found a long tube which he inserted down the man's throat, flooded the stomach with water, gave the patient a shot of morphine and then suggested he lean over the porch railing. Sure enough, the man gave a heave and a quart of water came shooting out, carrying the skin with it.

All through the summer and fall Brinkley practiced medicine in the hills, earning a horse, some sheep, calves, pigs, dogs, moonshine and eighty-five dollars. Realizing he could never get back to medical school with these wages, he made other plans. Once again using his Western Union connections, Brinkley left, ending up in St. Louis, Missouri, where there were three medical schools.

He obtained a job at Southern Railroad and worked there until he heard that an undergraduate physician could receive a medical license in Tennessee. So off he went. He passed the exam, earned a license and landed in Dandridge, Tennessee, where he saw an advertisement for a Knoxville medical group seeking a physician. Not understanding that advertising doctors were frowned upon by the medical establishment, he applied and was accepted.

When his name appeared with the advertising doctors, Brinkley was promptly notified by the Tennessee Medical Board that unless he terminated his connection with the group, his license would be revoked. This was Brinkley's first lesson about dealing with organized medical power, but he needed to make a living, so he chose to stay, gathered his family around him (which now consisted of three daughters) and accepted a job with the advertising doctors in Chattanooga -- where for a third time his wife and children left. This time, Brinkley announced that either his wife understood his need to be a doctor or the marriage was over. She filed for divorce.

By 1913, Brinkley was again in Chicago trying to gain the coveted medical degree. Quite by accident he met Minnie Jones, the daughter of a physician, and they soon married. The couple saved their money and Brinkley went to Kansas City to complete his last year of medical school.

Upon graduation, Brinkley and his classmates were told they were now in a strange situation. As graduates of an eclectic school, the State Board of Health in Missouri would not permit graduates of non-traditional schools to take the state exam unless they paid $500. The fee for traditional school graduates was $25. The graduates decided to take the licensing exam in Arkansas rather than Missouri, and Brinkley passed. He then took the Tennessee exam again and was licensed in two states.

The newlywed Dr. and Mrs. Brinkley spent the next few years trying to find a proper place in which to practice medicine. At every place he stayed, Dr. Brinkley heard something surprising, and remembered it. While working with a group of surgeons employed as U.S. meat inspectors he learned they all believed the goat was the healthiest animal slaughtered. Never had they seen an infected goat; the animal did not carry any disease communicable to humans, and it seemed naturally immune to tuberculosis. Brinkley remembered.

After much searching and a short stint as an Army surgeon during World War I, Dr. Brinkley decided to locate a practice in Milford, Kansas. Mrs. Brinkley cried.

Sitting on the Republican River, Milford was a run-down town in the middle of cattle-raising country. The only large building on Main Street had originally been part of the 1904 World's Fair in St. Louis. It was moved to Milford, where it served as a hotel, saloon and gambling joint before being abandoned. The town's post office operated from behind the old bar, but the depot was a mile away, and the only other structures were a general store, a barber shop and a bank.

The Brinkleys set up housekeeping and a medical office, and one of the doctor's early patients was a farmer who lived four miles out of town. He sat and talked for a long time before getting around to his problem.

"There is something wrong with me," he said, "though to look at me you wouldn't judge it. I look husky, don't I?"

"You certainly do," replied the doctor.

"Now here's just the trouble. I'm forty-six. The old woman's forty-two. Our youngest is eighteen years old. For the last sixteen years we have not been able to have any children."

Brinkley's face crinkled with puzzled interest. "You mean —"

"All in. No pep. A flat tire. I've been to plenty of doctors about it, and spent wads of money on 'em, too, and not one of 'em has done me a mite of good."

As the conversation continued, the two talked about what hadn't helped, about their similar backgrounds on the farm, and then Dr. Brinkley said, "You've probably seen rams and buck goats. You wouldn't have any trouble if you had a pair of those buck glands in you."

"Well, why don't you put 'em in?" asked the farmer.

Brinkley eventually did perform the operation, but only if the farmer promised not to tell anyone. The operation was deemed successful -- at least by those involved, and within a couple of weeks, another Milford farmer appeared late one night to talk to the doctor.

"Doc, I got the same sort of kidney trouble Jake had. He said for me to tell you, and you'd understand. He said for you to do the same thing for me you did for him."

Thus began Dr. John Brinkley's reputation as a rejuvenator of men, as the physician who had found the fountain of youth. There were some early setbacks, though, such as the two young men from California who discovered an unpleasant side effect after their operations. They smelled bad, and the odor was strong. Brinkley traced the origin of the two enormous, vicious, long-horned billies used in the operations to a farmer who snickered, "Well, they were Angora billies, Doc. I thought any dang fool would know an Angora stinks to heaven."

After that Dr. Brinkley carefully commissioned only milk varieties of goats, Toggenbergs, Nubians and Saanans, and his clientele grew. Soon the doctor realized he needed a hospital, so he built one and in the process gave Milford sidewalks, electricity and city water. The no-place town in the middle of Kansas became a popular railroad destination.

One of the reasons for the growth of Dr. Brinkley's practice was that he had learned the importance of advertising. He hired an expert who agreed Brinkley was no ordinary doctor. He had begun to see himself as exceptional, thus beyond the restraints applied to other physicians. Who cared if the A.M.A. disapproved of advertising? Certainly not his publicist. Brinkley's surgeries were made for the tabloids.

Newspapers across the country carried story after story of patients who returned home to sire children. Most of the articles were supplied by Brinkley's writers. The advertising expert had shown Brinkley that he had a commodity to sell that no other hospital in the country could offer — the elixir of eternal youth!

Photographs of him hugging one of the miracle children born after gland surgery were printed everywhere, and Brinkley expanded his marketing strategies. He produced a booklet about his surgery, about warning signs that surgery was needed, about the implications concerning prostate problems, and he began to idealize the advantages of prolonged life. The wise judge could stay on the bench; the honest policeman could be saved for further duty. Just think if the lives of men like John D. Rockefeller, William Shakespeare and Darwin had been extended.

By 1923 his hospital was full. Patients often arrived under false names, but they kept coming. Some well-known clients, such as Dr. J.J. Tobias, Chancellor of the Chicago Law School, allowed Brinkley to use their names in stories and photographs. The only problem with coming to Milford for rejuvenation was Milford. There was nothing to do in the town. As many as five-hundred people a day flocked to the goat-gland Mecca, crowding into the town's one restaurant, sleeping in cars because there was no hotel and having nothing to do as they waited for an operation or recuperated.

Brinkley had heard about a new gadget called radio, so he decided to establish a radio station which would entertain his patients, and, of course, it didn't hurt that the airways were a totally free form of advertising. Radio KFKB, letters which Brinkley alternately said meant "Kansas First, Kansas Best" or "Kansas Folks Know Best," ran a daily fare of medical programs, live music and health hints. Always open to a new idea, Brinkley agreed to a young teacher's request to offer something educational, and French language instruction was heard along with farm market reports, the "Tell Me a Story Lady" and Dr. Brinkley's "Medical Question Box."

KFKB was broadcasting well before there was a federal regulatory commission, and Brinkley's station could be heard as early as 5 a.m. and as late as 11 p.m. Radio brought out Brinkley's strongest talents. Like hundreds of others across the nation, Brinkley sold prepared tonics to his listeners. Originally he prepared and shipped a Special Gland Emulsion by mail order, but as he added more medicines, such as Caprikol, his resourcefulness and creativity flowered. His list of prescriptions were coded by number and sent to pharmacists who could buy the tonics, and the only expectation was a dollar kick-back for each prescription sold. As the scheme took root, Brinkley organized druggists nationally, and during his radio talk shows he would read a listener's letter, explain the complaint and then recommend a medication. Of course, listeners often felt similar complaints or symptoms, so they listened when the doctor said, "Take Women's Tonic Number fifty, sixty-seven and sixty-one...This combination will do for you what you desire...after three months' persistent use," or "For kidney stones, try Number eighty and fifty." All listeners had to do was go to the local drugstore and buy themselves the proper cure.

Price cutters were not allowed to sell the numbered prescriptions, and some researchers have maintained that the medicine scheme brought Brinkley far more money than did the goat gland operations. He had found a way to cross the patent medicine shelf and the prescription counter.

Daily, Brinkley mailed out literature, and he received hundreds of letters each day in return. An unquestioned forerunner of today's mass marketing techniques, Brinkley sent out newsletters, brochures, booklets about his hospital, his surgeries, suspicious symptoms, pictures, pamphlets and always stories about "the boy from the hills." As he made more and more money, Brinkley found more and more ways to spend it. He purchased land, bought his wife a fur coat and a sports car, gave himself diamond rings and a diamond stickpin, even bought seven-thousand acres of land near where he was born. A fascinating aspect of Brinkley's life is that he enjoyed seeing his name on his possessions, so even today the artful rock entrance to the tree farm and nursery that once was his mountain farm in Tuckasegee, N.C. bears the

106

full name Dr. John R. Brinkley, spelled out in white quartz rocks. He always put his name on his hospitals and loved seeing the initial "B" or his last name on the hubcaps of his car, his luggage, his yacht and all his printed matter. Now a national figure, if he decided to spend a few days at the Waldorf Astoria in New York, all he had to do was make a few phone calls and a press conference was available. He managed to parlay his original medical licenses into several more licenses using reciprocity agreements between states. He was awarded an honorary medical degree from the Kansas City College of Medicine and Surgery in recognition of his work in public health, which he took to Italy and turned into a medical degree from the Royal University of Pavia. Then he went to England which usually recognized Italian degrees, and he came home saying he had British recognition, too. It was just too much for the American medical establishment. He had not broken a law, but the clever, resourceful mountain boy had certainly used whatever was at hand.

In 1930, the Kansas Medical Society filed a complaint with the Kansas State Board of Medical Registration and Examination against Dr. Brinkley. *The Kansas City Star* also took aim and began an investigative report about the strange yet flourishing hospital in the tiny hamlet of Milford. As the Kansas Medical Society built its case, the American Medical Association threw its weight into the fight, calling Brinkley's work "blatant quackery." Brinkley filed several lawsuits and never lost his equilibrium, but his enemies countered with questions about his radio license.

Brinkley was summoned to Washington, D.C., to appear before the Federal Radio Commission to answer complaints that he used the airways for reasons contrary to the public good. He headed for his radio microphone and asked supporters to go with him to Washington. They could present a living petition protesting the cancellation of his license, and he did not forget to mention that in a recent nationwide radio station popularity contest, KFKB had been the winner with 356, 827 votes. His opponent's station WDAF, *The Kansas City Star's* station, received only 10,000 votes. Obviously the people were with Brinkley.

When he testified in Washington, dozens of people from the North Carolina county where he had grown up testified to his education, reliability and general good character. And he scored more points with the American public when he was asked, "What kinds of entertainment do you give your listeners?"

"The sort of entertainment they like," he replied. Committee members' responses indicated they preferred the music of the cultural East, and Brinkley wrote that it was obvious "they regarded the people west of the Mississippi as morons and ignoramuses." Forget the Eastern power brokers, Brinkley was a man of the people.

As the assaults and criticisms — persecution some called it — continued, Brinkley offered to perform a transplant operation before members of the Kansas Medical Board and other "distinguished observers." No one who watched that day doubted the doctor's nerve. As he worked, he lectured, and soft music from the radio station floated into the operating room. The board members retired to consider the matter, and Brinkley believed that not only he but "the public mind had been ready for an acquittal." It did not happen. Two days later the Board revoked Dr. Brinkley's license to practice medicine in Kansas.

It was only the beginning of the bad news. His prized diploma from the Royal University of Pavia had been revoked, decided, Brinkley maintained, by Mussolini after he was pressured by the American Medical Association. And he lost his radio license with the additional nuisance of legal prohibitions which forbade the sale of the station, too.

If anyone believed Brinkley was beaten, they were wrong.

Brinkley leased a telephone line from The American Telegraph and Telephone Company to a powerful radio station on the Mexican side of the Rio Grande River, station XER. Now he phoned in his broadcasts to Mexico, and since the station was outside the jurisdiction of the Federal Radio Commission, no one could stop him from talking directly to the people.

As the opening bars of "America," Brinkley's theme song, opened his daily radio program, the doctor's familiar voice was heard across the United States and into Canada. Brinkley simply turned up the voltage as he continued his talks about health, but now he also spent time describing his recent persecutions. His sense of mission, the same drive he'd had as a youngster, was still with him and probably stronger. His calling now went beyond medicine — he was a leader and spokesman for all those ordinary people forgotten by big government.

When a supporter suggested he run for governor of Kansas, Brinkley liked the idea. It fit his calling, and it would allow him to prove himself to his enemies. When he said he might consider running for President of the United States — in jest, he always insisted — both the Democratic and Republican National Committees were surprised. Sure, Brinkley had always been an issue, but now it was obvious he could be a contender, especially given the positive grassroots response.

Brinkley never entered national politics, but on September 30, 1930, when he announced he would run as an independent candidate for the governorship of Kansas, it was the beginning of one of the weirdest campaigns known. The deadline had passed for Brinkley to get his name on the ballot, which he knew. He would have to rely totally upon write-in votes, and he had no organization, just his name and reputation. But just as he had introduced new ideas into radio programming and marketing of medicines, Brinkley changed the way American politicians campaigned.

Naturally he used radio extensively, but he also used his private plane to zip him across the state so he could talk directly to voters. He bought a sound truck which drove from town to town, stopping in the busiest sections. The back of the truck was lowered, electricity hooked up to the microphones and Brinkley took the stage. He hired cheerleaders and musicians to help draw a crowd. Nurses passed out lollipops and balloons. Mrs. Brinkley and their son, Johnny Boy, joined the campaign trail. Johnny Boy was often persuaded to greet young friends or to sing a sweet ditty. At formal debates or forums, the Brinkleys stood by the exit to shake the hand of each person leaving, and Mrs. Brinkley sometimes gave away flowers. Always, the doctor told his Horatio Alger life story. The campaign strategies he developed have been repeatedly copied. He mixed the story of his life and troubles with a dose of "trust--me; I'm--just--like--you" rhetoric, and it worked.

At every stop he reminded voters that the establishment did not want him to win. The rules had been changed so that no longer did the voter's intent count; now the only votes which would be awarded to Dr. Brinkley were the ones which read "J.R. Brinkley." Other variations of his name would be thrown out. Not John R. Brinkley, not Mr. Brinkley, not Dr. Brinkley. And each write-in voter had to also make a cross in the square after "J.R. Brinkley."

"I get thousands of letters every day. These people who write to me are intelligent people. They are for me and they know enough to know how to write my name on the ballot," he told voters. His simple slogan — "Clean Out, Clean Up and Keep Kansas Clean" — and his dramatic campaigning were not matched by his two younger opponents. By October, politicians in both parties were near panic. Polls indicated people would vote for Brinkley "by the thousands." In the midst of the confusion, Brinkley's message was clear. "The Democrats are saying the Republicans are crooked and no good and should be thrown out of office. The Republicans say the same thing about the Democrats. Why shouldn't you vote for me? I belong to neither party."

On Election Day 1930, amplifiers near voting places reminded voters "Vote for J.R. Brinkley and mark the cross in the square. Write the letter 'J,' the letter 'R' then B-R-I-N-K-L-E-Y."

When the voting was over, more than 50,000 votes for Brinkley were voided because the ballot did not meet the strict rule about the candidate's name. Brinkley estimated he would have received 239,000 votes if the intent of the voters had been considered; it wasn't. The Democratic candidate took the election with 217,171 votes, but three counties in Oklahoma voted for Brinkley! Apparently his message had been received loud and clear by radio listeners in Oklahoma, and voters in three counties had followed the balloting instructions even though Brinkley was not running for an office in their state.

110

Privately, everyone agreed the election was Brinkley's, and he would have been moving into the governor's mansion if his name had been printed on the ballot. No one demanded a recount, though. The Republican loser's tallies were close to the Democratic winner's, but neither party wanted a recount for fear Dr. Brinkley's totals would increase. Brinkley made it known that he'd be delighted to run again in '32--and the next time he'd be sure to get his name on the ballot.

And he did. The campaign truck was in service again, the singers and showmanship of the first campaign were used again. But Brinkley finished third with 244,607 votes. So he devoted his time to expanding the radio station across the Rio Grande at Villa Acuna, Mexico.

A building was erected for the station and just as he had transformed Milford, Dr. Brinkley began changing Del Rio, Texas, the closest American town to Villa Acuna and "XER, the Sunshine Station Between the Nations." The Chamber of Commerce welcomed him with eager arms as XER spewed forth programs featuring the good doctor, his medical practice and a variety of live performers.

The Milford practice was transferred to the Roswell Hotel at Del Rio and later a Brinkley Hospital was built for all those who continued to need one or more of the doctor's special surgeries. By this time, Dr. Brinkley had dropped the goat gland transplants in favor of alternative methods, but the nation would forever call him "The Goat Gland King."

Listed in his repertoire of surgeries was the newly available Average Man's Treatment, another unique Brinkley bit of marketing. Long before deluxe editions became common practice, Brinkley offered two kinds of treatment: the Average Man's Treatment and the Business Man's Treatment. The Average Man's Treatment did not necessarily mean a patient would be seen by Dr. Brinkley himself. The deluxe version was given personally by the doctor and carried a lifetime guarantee, the privilege of writing to the doctor and free urine checks every six months.

Dr. Brinkley began selling copies of his version of his life's story, *The Story of a Man,* for one dollar, and he continually upped the wattage at XER until it reached five-hundred-thousand watts. He acquired more yachts, more Mexican radio stations, more diamond rings and more cars. For the occasional challenges, he always found an answer. When Mexican authorities threatened to force him out of XER, he developed a plan. He would simply put the station on his new one-hundred-fifty foot yacht and continue broadcasting from sea. The plan was never carried out because the problem was resolved and the station returned to the airways as XERA.

Despite all the trappings of wealth, Dr. Brinkley remained a country boy in more than his own imagination. Loaded with diamonds and expensive clothes, he continued to chew on toothpicks in public, and he combed his beard whenever he felt the urge. He always carried an ear pick in his vest pocket only now the tool was gold.

He claimed never to keep books, even as he opened another hospital, yet he purchased a goat farm in Oklahoma, a ranch in Texas, a Lockheed Electra plane, more than a dozen Cadillacs, several oil leases, two citrus groves and much more. A well-known story about Brinkley's bookkeeping practices occurred while he was ordering the large towers for XER. "Now how much will that be?" he asked.

"Thirty-eight-thousand dollars," was the reply. Brinkley pulled out his wallet and counted out thirty-eight one-thousand-dollar bills.

Once the Brinkley home was completed at Del Rio, and the town had received numerous gifts from the doctor, the doctor's never-ending stream of literature urged readers "to come for a visit." When he wasn't dressed in his yachting clothes and headed for the docks or checking on something at the hospital, he rested at home, a luxurious residence surrounded by sixteen lush acres in the middle of a parched Texas landscape. There he could play with his Galapagos tortoises or his flock of penguins, smell his roses or ponder the twenty-foot bronze Winged Victory in the front yard. He always said he had picked the statue as his grave marker. Other statuary in the yard included an eight-foot-long Roman she-wolf of the Romulus and Remus legend. At night the "home place" was lit up by flashing neon lights that played across the lily pool and two fountains. If a visitor was unsure what he was seeing, a fluorescent "Dr. Brinkley" lit up the base of the fountains. Brinkley often said his only regret about the estate "was that I cannot bring the little log cabin that was my mother's home down here with me and re-erect it on my premises."

Life was good, though. He sailed around the world, attended several international Rotary conventions (he was an enthusiastic Rotarian), received invitations to the White House and always appeared surprised when some supporter suggested he run for President.

Success and the public spotlight did bring some problems. Brinkley discovered he was being imitated by other physicians who charged far less and the federal government began to examine his life with scrutiny. He decided to relocate to Little Rock, Arkansas, and shortly thereafter the Internal Revenue Service said he owed $200,000 in back taxes. The financial wrangling went on for years, and it became obvious that for a man who disdained strenuous bookkeeping he had listened to some good financial advice from somewhere. A great deal of his holdings were in family members' names or tied up in partnerships. As his money problems dragged along, creditors who would have once been patient now demanded immediate payment. It's hard to believe the doctor found himself financially embarrassed, but he filed for bankruptcy on January 31, 1941.

The diamond jewelry he wore would have fed several families for several years, but even when he entered the courtroom to plead bankruptcy, he could not leave the jewelry at home. Besides, when the lawyers did turn up something of value there was always doubt about who owned it. Frequently the money was originally Mrs. Brinkley's or the property in Johnny Boy's name or mortgaged. If he hadn't outsmarted the IRS, he certainly gave them a good hunt.

In the spring of 1941, Dr. Brinkley suffered the first of several heart attacks. In August a clot blocked the large artery in his leg. He was taken to the hospital "a very sick man." Four weeks later, while he was convalescing, he had two more heart attacks. About the same time, the Post Office

113

Department filed an old complaint against him for fraud, one dating back to his goat-gland days decades earlier. A federal fugitive warrant for the doctor was issued as he lay in bed, unable to run anywhere.

John Romulus Brinkley died on May 27, 1942, before the scheduled trial date concerning the Post Office complaint. He died as a nurse raised him to give him a drink of water. His life had been a fifty-six year roller-coaster ride, one of overwork, constant litigation, nervy showmanship with some Brinkley brinkmanship thrown in. He'd known both small and large pressures, successes and defeats.

When he died, the life of this particular poor mountain boy had affected more of American life than probably even he realized. Changes in broadcasting, licensing procedures for physicians, marketing practices, voting and balloting laws, and political campaigning all happened because of Brinkley's controversial life. Whether one believed he was a self-promoting egomaniac or the embodiment of the American success story, those who actually met the man usually agreed with the Del Rio businessman who said, "I don't know what there was about him. You might laugh about all of it. But when you were talking with him — well, you just forgot everything .... You couldn't help liking him."

N.A.

NOTE: Dr. Brinkley's grave in Memphis, TN., is marked by the bronze Winged Victory statue just as he planned.

Sources for this story include Clement Wood's *The Life of a Man: Biography of John R. Brinkley*, Brinkley's brochures, other Brinkley publications, and an interview with Harry Cagle, taped in 1986 by Jan Davidson. The tape is on file at the Mountain Heritage Center, Western Carolina University at Cullowhee.

Entrance to Dr. Brinkley's mountain farm

Newspaper advertisement for Albert Teaster's performance.

THEY SHALL
TAKE UP SERPENTS

Sunday evening, August 5, 1934:

As Albert Teaster, thirty-nine, self-ordained minister for the Church of God, raised his eyes from his text, aware of the hush that had suddenly fallen on his little congregation, he saw the man with the box. He stood for a moment in the doorway and then came forward and knelt. Smiling, he indicated the box and placed it on a bench beside Teaster.

"You say a man that's got the faith can pick up serpents and they won't harm him." The man smiled at the minister. "Open up that box and let's see."

It was not a pleasant smile. Teaster saw the scorn in his face as the man stood to walk away.

"Mockers and doubters," Teaster told his friends that morning. "They sneer when I preach because I'm not ordained. Today, they intend to test me."

Indeed, they did. The box held a five-foot diamond-back rattler. Teaster surveyed his kneeling audience. Approximately two dozen members of Cullowhee Mountain Church of God returned his gaze. It was a hot evening and the minister noted the stillness in the little cabin that served as a church, the church itself having burned to the ground two weeks previously. The congregation had seen the box carried into the room, and Teaster sensed they knew what was in it. After all, they had all been present two weeks ago when he had read from Luke:

And he said unto them. Go ye into all the world, and preach the gospel to every creature. He that believeth and is baptized shall be saved; but he that believeth not shall be damned. And these signs shall follow them that believe; in my name shall they cast out devils; they shall speak with new tongues; they shall take up serpents; and if they drink any deadly thing, it shall not hurt them; they shall lay hands on the sick and they shall recover. So then, after the Lord had spoken to them, he was received up into heaven, and sat on the right hand of God. And they went forth and preached everywhere, the Lord working with them and conforming the word with signs following.

Reading the passage to his little flock, Teaster had been moved to say that should the occasion present itself, he would gladly undergo such tests. It was then the mocker spoke:

"Ye would let a snake bite ye, brother Teaster?"

The minister had said he would. Spurred on by the mocker's scornful laugh, Teaster stated that less than two years previously his wife had refused to accept medical care and had told her husband to throw out all her medicine. "I will put my faith in Jesus," she said. She died shortly afterwards due to complications attending childbirth. So it was that Teaster had been moved to become an exhorter and testifier for the Church of God. Thus, two weeks before he had told his membership that he would welcome an opportunity to prove his faith.

I won't seek out a test," he had said, "but if it comes to me, I'll stand fast."

Had they come to worship or to see what he would do? Teaster tore a slat from the top of the box revealing the snake. Looking about him, he saw the expectant faces, waiting. The serpent's body shifted in the box, the flat head floated upwards, the tongue flicking, the eyes alert, deadly. Teaster reached for the snake.

"I grabbed it in the middle," he said later, "so it could bite me if it wanted to." The rattler's response was immediate. With blinding quickness, the mouth gaped and struck. Members of the congregation later noted they

118

saw green spurts of poison as the snake sank its fangs into Teaster's right hand. Dropping the snake, the minister stood for a moment staring at the punctures in the web of skin between his thumb and index finger. Then, he deliberately stooped and seized the snake again, raising it above his head. The snake struck twice more before Teaster threw it from him and stumbled across the floor and out of the cabin.

In the dim lamp-light, Teaster's flock looked nervously about for the snake. Panic ensued and many fled into the night. Eventually, word spread that the snake had crawled through the open doorway vanishing into the underbrush, and the congregation returned to tend the minister.

Later, witnesses described Teaster's reaction to the snake-bite, stating that the pain was so great, Teaster momentarily lost his composure. "He fell and rolled in the grass outside the church," said one church member. "But in a minute, he returned to the church and calmly told us that God would take care of him. He told the man that had mocked him that if he died, he 'would die trusting in Jesus.' Within moments, his arm began to swell. Several church members volunteered to go for medical assistance. "I'll have no doctors," said Teaster. "God will take care of me." The minister managed to walk to a nearby cabin where he was placed in bed. In a short time, his condition worsened.

"My tongue swelled until I couldn't speak," said Teaster five days later. "I couldn't see and my teeth locked." According to Bud Bryson, one member of the group, the members of the church gathered about the bed and prayed for several hours. At one point, Teaster was placed on a pallet and carried into a field where he was told to get up and walk. He managed to take about thirty steps before he was carried back to the house. The prayers continued until almost everyone, including Teaster, fell asleep. "I prayed until I couldn't stand up straight afterwards," said Bryson.

Teaster was finally returned to his own home, a three-room cabin where he lay near death for three days. During this time, friends and neighbors repeatedly attempted to persuade him to accept medical attention. Barely able to whisper, Teaster refused all remedies, including corn liquor from a nearby still. "Alcohol just makes the snake madder," said Teaster. When a friend walked seven miles to the minister's cabin with a homemade remedy containing a native plant known as "Rattlesnake Master" and milk, the stricken man told his friends he was being treated by the greatest of all doctors, Jesus Christ.

Two days later, Frank Allen, a deputy sheriff who lived in Cashiers, visited Teaster and questioned him about his reasons for allowing the snake to bite him. Allen shared the incident with John Parris, a young man who was to become a noted mountain writer. The story seized Parris' imagination; he immediately reported it to the Asheville *Citizen-Times*, the Associated Press and the United Press. Recalling the incident in 1991, Parris wrote, "The next morning at 6 o'clock, I was awakened by a telephone call from the Charlotte Bureau of the Associated Press." The story had received front page coverage throughout the country and in Europe. "They wanted me to interview Teaster and get a picture."

Parris borrowed a camera and went to see the stricken man. Five days had lapsed since Teaster was bitten. Parris later wrote, "I found him lying on a bed in a little room in the back of the house. He still wore the blue serge trousers and the white shirt he had worn on Sunday night, August 5, when he was bitten, but the right sleeve had been cut away at the shoulder." Parris noted that the man's arm was swollen as big as a stove pipe. Parris told Teaster that he wanted a picture but Teaster would have to come out on the porch in the sunlight. The preacher hesitated, saying he needed to pray over it, and Parris went outside and waited. Teaster and his chief saint, a man named Lindsay Coggins, prayed for some fifteen minutes. Teaster came out on the porch and Parris took a photograph that appeared in every daily paper served by the Associated Press.

Perhaps the most intriguing aspect of this story is not Teaster's ordeal, but the public's reaction to it. Telegrams arrived with offers for speaking engagements. Pathe News and Paramount News asked for a filmed interview.

The bewildered mountain preacher found himself thrust into the harsh public eye. Was this yet another test? The Reverend Teaster prayed over it.

On the Sunday following, Teaster returned to his flock, walking six miles to the home of Mark Coggins where he preached from the front porch. He said God had provided him with an opportunity to spread the word of Jesus. He would talk to the movie people, and he asked his congregation to share the experience with him. Then he would venture into that loud, seething world beyond Cullowhee Mountain, and John Parris would go with him.

Pathe News filmed Teaster and his congregation as they performed a strange ritual. Singing, dancing and "speaking in tongues," they kissed the minister's swollen arm as the filming crew thrust microphones towards the chanting, whirling flock. "Comoco, comoco, toeee, toeee!"

Afterwards, Teaster walked the six miles home.

In Asheville, the Plaza Theatre asked Teaster to speak from their stage in conjunction with the Pathe News showing (at 3:30, 7:30 and 9:30 p.m.). At the same time, Paramount News was running their version of Teaster and the snake at the Imperial Theatre. Large crowds attended both films despite the fact that Tom Mix was in town with the Sam Dill Circus.

In Charlotte, the minister appeared in hat and tie to speak over a nation-wide and Canadian CBS radio broadcast. Patiently, he repeated his belief that God wanted him to let the snake bite him so that he could be afforded this opportunity to spread the word of Jesus. Certainly, he was being provided with ample opportunities to do so.

Telegrams continued to pour in: offers for speaking engagements, tours and revivals. The Church of God in Akron, Ohio, and a nation-wide tour which would begin in Baltimore, Maryland, wanted him. Teaster was assured that he was needed — that the world was eager to learn of his experience and his faith.

Back in the mountain fastness of western North Carolina, the Reverend E.D. Hopkins of East La Porte made a public announcement. Albert Teaster's experience had qualified him for official recognition as an active minister of the Holiness Church. In effect, the Rev. Hopkins considered Teaster ordained and expressed his hope that Teaster would return to assume his pastoral duties.

Except for a few short visits to his family on holidays, Teaster did not return. Eventually even the brief visits stopped. He gave his soul to the world beyond the North Carolina mountains, traveling from city to city with revivalists and chautauquas. Again and again he stood on stages, his right hand raised as he indicated the punctures, and told how he resisted pleas from others to bring him medical attention. "I told them I had the greatest doctor in the world, already," he would say again and again. "His name is Jesus Christ."

Within days, public reaction cooled. A noted physician in Asheville published a letter in the *Citizen* that said people rarely die of rattlesnake bites if they have appropriate medical treatment. He said Teaster's refusal to do so caused him extensive suffering but probably did not endanger his life. Some editorials praised the minister's faith, but asserted the belief that such demonstrations were foolish and perhaps criminal. Others pointedly questioned his sanity. The editor of the Jackson County *Journal* told his readers that Teaster was not a native of Jackson County, having moved there four years previously. The following week, the editor of the Transylvania *Times* noted that Jackson County's *Journal* seemed to be ashamed of the snake-handling minister and concluded, "We don't blame you! If we had such an idiot in Transylvania, we would blame his reason for being born into the world on some other 'section.'"

On August 31, a few days before Teaster left the mountains, the editor of the *Journal* reported the following anecdote:

> *Saw Albert Teester in a store, preparing to go to Akron.*
> *He was buying a pair of suspenders. Laughed myself*
> *sick wondering why he should need 'em since it does*
> *look like a faith strong enough to cure a rattlesnake bite*
> *could hold up a pair of trousers.*

To look at Teaster's photograph now — that photograph made by John Parris with a borrowed Kodak — prompts endless questions. What was he thinking, this man with the haunted eyes and the swollen arm? Certainly it is the photograph of a haggard, sick man, but there is something else. Albert Teaster looks bewildered. Staring at the camera, he seems to be saying, "Would someone tell me what is happening?"

Fifty-seven years later, John Parris retold the story in a two-part article for the Asheville *Citizen-Times*. "For me, the Albert Teaster story brought a job offer from United Press that same August," he said. "I left the mountains for a newspaper career that took me to Raleigh and to New York and to London, and finally back to the mountains where I started."

Albert Teaster died in 1967 at the home of a daughter in Statesville, N.C.

G.C.

ADDENDUM

Of all the material in this book, the story of Albert Teaster, the Cullowhee snake-handler, is subject to more conflicting information than any other. The memories of eyewitnesses and numerous newspaper accounts are filled with conflicting details. Teaster's name is repeatedly misspelled, and the details regarding his family life are remarkably contradictory. Examples of the confusion are these: Did the snake-handling take place in a church or a residence being used as a church? Was the snake in a black box or an orange crate? Did Teaster wear a short-sleeve or long-sleeve shirt? Did the snake get away or was it killed? Did Teaster ever return to Jackson County? In all of the foregoing questions, the sources seem equally divided in every instance. In writing Teaster's story, the author has attempted to pick the most credible source in each instance. For example, in all photographs of Teaster, he is shown wearing a long-sleeve shirt with one sleeve torn away to accommodate his swollen arm, and he is repeatedly described as wearing the same shirt he wore when he was bitten. Despite the commonly reported belief that he never returned to Jackson County, the Asheville *Citizen* for 1934 carries a number of articles dealing with Teaster's return to visit his family.

As is frequently the case with stories that catch the public's interest, Albert Teaster has two stories: one is fact and the other is myth. As time passes, the gulf between the two will increase and minor inconsistencies will become major ones. In one sense, both are valid. The first will satisfy the historian; the second will please the storyteller.

THE GHIGHAU
(THE BELOVED WOMAN)

A great deal of foolishness has been written about Nancy Ward, the Cherokee "Beloved Woman." Like hundreds of Native Americans whose only biographers were white, she frequently emerges clothed in European culture and values. Many historians place undue emphasis on the allegedly aristocratic role of the "Ghighau," and since several contemporaries who met Nancy Ward described her demeanor as commanding and assertive, later writers have not hesitated to call her by such embarrassing names as "The Cherokee Pocahontas," "Princess" or "Prophetess," and even "Chieftainess."

A novel allegedly based on her life has Nancy behaving like a Bronte heroine as she rushes back and forth under the cover of night to meet one of her two lovers. (She is torn between the world of English nobility and the natural world of her Cherokee lover who always greets her by the moon-lit waterfall by saying "Ugg! Ugg!")

The real Ghighau who emerges from historical accounts bears no resemblance to the fairy-like creature who was a direct descendant of Cherokee royalty. She was much more.

Like that of most of her contemporaries, the date of Nancy Ward's birth is unknown. Circa 1737-38, she was born at Chota, the "Mother Town of the Cherokees," the daughter of a Delaware Chief and Tame Doe, the sister of the great Cherokee leader, Attakullakulla. Most of her early life was spent at Chota, and she witnessed many of the radical alterations in Cherokee culture which were born of necessity. During her lifetime, her people were faced with the possibility of extinction.

Many of the early white visitors to Chota and other villages in eastern Tennessee commented on the strong matriarchial character of Cherokee government. Women acted and spoke as equals to men, and English officers often spoke contemptuously of the Cherokees' "petticoat" government. Blood lines were traced through the mother, and warriors from other tribes, such as Nancy Ward's father, were required to adopt his wife's clan. Ownership of property was largely controlled by women, and early traders noted that divorce was usually instigated by the wife. In addition, women were represented at council meetings and did not hesitate to question the decision of the tribal leaders.

This was the culture that nurtured Nanyehi, the young woman who was to become Nancy Ward. She was accustomed to hearing women speak their minds, and as a young woman, she sat with the women who composed the Women's Council as they discussed the problems facing the tribe. Increasingly, the most common problem was the steady encroachment of white settlers.

Married at an early age, Nanyehi accompanied her warrior husband, Kingfisher, on raids against the Muskogeans (Creeks) in northern Georgia. The Muskogeans had invaded Cherokee territory and had announced their intention of remaining. Kingfisher hated the invaders and as this thirty-year conflict dragged on, his young wife came to share his enmity. In the last encounter which came to be known as the "Battle of Taliwa" in 1775, Kingfisher and his young wife accompanied a five-hundred-man war party into the heart of the contested land. According to the oft-repeated story, Nanyehi assisted her husband by chewing the bullets used in his gun, thereby producing a projectile that would mangle and tear the flesh of the enemy.

While thus occupied she saw her husband fall, mortally wounded. Rising from the protection offered by a fallen tree, Nanyehi picked up her husband's rifle and began firing at the enemy. In fact, oral tradition of the

Cherokees claims that she was responsible for turning the tide of the battle. Firing with deadly accuracy and advancing steadily on a confused enemy, she drove the Muskogeans from the land. Thus ended a feud that had begun in 1715! The Cherokee war party returned repeating the story of her valor.

And so it was that Nanyehi became "Ghighau" — the Most Honored or Beloved Woman. It is especially interesting to note that in Cherokee tradition, the honor of being chosen "Ghighau" was normally reserved for a woman whose long life of service to her people made her eligible. However, when Nanyehi was acclaimed deserving of this honor by the Chiefs, the council and the clan spokesmen, she was still a teenager!

Since the honor awarded Nanyehi was an acknowledgement that the Great Spirit would speak through her, Nanyehi was in effect the most powerful tribal officer at Chota. Henceforth, she would sit by the Peace Chief in times of peace, and the Red Chief in times of war. She would sit in the holy area next to the ceremonial fire, and if she chose to do so, she could overrule any decision made by the council. As a token of her power, she was given a swan's wing which was attached to her left arm between the elbow and wrist. In order to render judgment, command attention or defy a council decision, she had merely to raise it. Her term of office was for life.

Nanyehi had two children by Kingfisher — Catherine and Little Fellow. Sometime in the 1750s, she met an English trader named Bryant Ward. The story that has been passed down over the years says she was married to Ward in a civil ceremony. One child, named Elizabeth, was born of this union. Henceforth, Nanyehi used her English name, Nancy Ward.

Very little is known about Bryant Ward. Several historians note that he had served in the British army and that he was "a descendant of Irish Nobility." His first wife had died in Ireland, and after coming to America as a trader, he married Nanyehi, probably because the Cherokees refused to allow white men to remain on tribal land for extended periods unless they married into the tribe. In 1764, John Ward, Bryant's son by his first marriage, arrived in Cherokee country searching for his father. He learned that Bryant and Nancy were separated and Bryant had gone south. After meeting his

127

stepmother, who was living in what one historian called "barbaric splendor," John decided to remain in Cherokee country. He afterwards married the seventeen-year-old daughter of a Scot named McDaniel who had married a full-blood. John and Katie Ward had eight children and remained in Cherokee country for the rest of their lives.

After becoming the Blessed Woman, Nancy Ward became a woman of substance. There is a significant reason for her success. As the years passed, the Cherokees found themselves dealing with a brutal reality. The growing flood of white settlers could not be halted, and it was becoming increasingly evident that continued resistance was futile. Like other Cherokee leaders, Nancy Ward came to the conclusion that the survival of her people depended, not on resistance and warfare, but on acculturation. If the Cherokees were to survive, they must learn to live in the white man's world. The Ghighau urged her people to adjust. Put down the rifle and the tomahawk. Take up the plow and the spindle. She became a living example of the philosophy she preached.

Nancy Ward befriended settlers. She became interested in livestock and farming. Over a decade she amassed a sizable herd of horses and cattle. She studied commerce and trade. In a short time Nancy Ward and all those who saw the wisdom of her advice began to prosper. In her role as Ghighau, she spoke in council about the benefits of the white man's way. When young warriors stood to denounce yet another betrayal by the British or the Americans, she rose to say that the fighting must stop. "You cannot win," she said. "If you fight, we will cease to be." The young men shook their heads in anger. One of them stood time and time again to say, "No! I am a warrior, and I will not milk cows and plow cotton." He went on to say the only way, the only honorable way, was to drive the white man from the land. He said he would rather die fighting than to die "by inches" in the white man's world. He was Dragging Canoe, the warrior son of Attakullakulla.

In Spring 1776, the English came to the Cherokees with a proposal. Forget our past differences. Forget the broken treaties and the burned villages. We will join with you to drive the Americans from your land. Help us and we will be generous. Much of your land will be returned. Then, representatives from other tribes began arriving at Chota. Iroquois, Mohawk, Delaware, Ottawas, Shawnee and Mingo. Join our federation, they said. Together we can defeat the white man. A Grand Council was called at Chota and each of the members of the federation spoke.

It seems safe to assume that Nancy Ward was there. Certainly, there were many who spoke against the federation. "We are just beginning to learn to live together," they said. But Dragging Canoe spoke contemptuously of the men who were too old to hunt or fight. He recalled the day in March 1775 when the old chiefs had been tricked into signing the infamous Transylvania Agreement whereby the Cherokees had lost all of their eastern hunting grounds, including Kentucky. Not again, he said. "There is nothing left but the bloody path."

In the days following his announcement, Dragging Canoe found himself facing unexpected resistance from his allies. Spokesmen for the British began to arrive asking Dragging Canoe to wait. We must plan a concerted effort, they said. The American Revolution had begun, and the fury of the Americans had astonished the British. Seeing their forces in retreat they advised Dragging Canoe to await future instructions. The impatient warrior noted that English traders were leaving Cherokee country in droves. When he demanded an explanation, they said they were off to plan strategy. "Patience," they said, as they took the road to Charleston. "We will be back."

Dragging Canoe decided not to wait. It was July 1776.

According to James Ramsey's *The Annals of Tennessee,* the settlers of Watauga had been lulled into a sense of false security. Their relationship with the Cherokees had been peaceable for more than seven years now. They were without forts or organized militia. It is for this reason that historians have traditionally credited Nancy Ward with saving the lives of the Wautagan settlers.

As Dragging Canoe planned his attack, Nancy Ward held her peace and listened. She learned that Dragging Canoe had contacted the Raven and

Chief Abram and developed a strategy. Dragging Canoe would attack the settlements along the Long Island and lower Virginia; Chief Abram would lead a war party through the Watauga Valley and Chief Raven would attack Carter's Valley. It was a good plan and with the element of surprise, it would work.

On July 8, about nine days before Dragging Canoe launched his attack, Nancy Ward sent Isaac Thomas and four white traders with messages warning the settlers along the Holston Valley of the impending raid. Nancy's warning, coming a few days after the discovery of the body of a murdered settler prompted the settlers to action. Women and children were sent to the nearest fort and additional forts and stockades were constructed. At Island Flats armed sharpshooters waited for Dragging Canoe.

Dragging Canoe's surprise attack was met by a withering barrage of gunfire. The young war chief fell, shot through the thigh, and was carried from the battlefield by his retreating men. When the Raven discovered that the settlers of Carter's Valley had been alerted, he split his forces into small bands and instructed them to loot and burn isolated farms. Chief Abram found the settlements in the Watauga Valley abandoned. Continuing on to Fort Watauga, the old chief laid seige to the fort. Two days later, he heard that a large American force was on its way. Discouraged by his lack of success and by the news that Dragging Canoe had been defeated, he halted the siege and turned toward home. Near Nolichucky, his braves captured Mrs. William Bean and a boy named Samuel Moore. Abram, frustrated by the fact that his attack had netted only a few murdered settlers, turned the boy over to his warriors. The boy was subjected to torture and burned at the stake. Mrs. Bean was questioned regarding Fort Henry's arms and provisions. Her information only served to depress Abram further. He ordered her imprisoned at the village of Toqua where plans were quickly made to burn her at the stake.

Hearing of Mrs. Bean's capture, Nancy Ward immediately went to Toqua where she discovered the captive already bound to a pole in the center of the village. Several warriors had just lit the fire. According to oral tradition, the Ghighau kicked the burning brands away, stomped out the flames and cut Mrs. Bean's bonds. Then, turning on the villagers, she asked when did Cherokee warriors sink so low as to resort to torturing women. "So long as I hold the title of Ghighau, no woman will be burned in a Cherokee village." Then, taking Mrs. Bean by the arm, she led her through the silent warriors.

There are other stories, of course. One of the most credible tells how Nancy Ward whispered to the captive as she was still tied to the pole, "Can you make butter and cheese?" The bewildered Mrs. Bean finally said she could. Then the Ghighau turned to the villagers and announced that the captive was a valuable source of information. She could teach the Ghighau household secrets and the Ghighau would teach them to others. Given Nancy Ward's commitment to learning to survive in the white world, this story has the ring of truth. In the following weeks, Mrs. Bean lived in the Ghighau's house in Chota, the town of Sanctuary. When the excitement subsided, Nancy Ward's son, Five Killer, and her brother, Long Fellow, accompanied Mrs. Bean back to her Watauga home. It is assumed that Nancy, who had an inordinate fondness for cows, learned to make butter and cheese. Most of her neighbors did not share her enthusiasm.

It is likely that the Ghighau's act of courage saved her family's life as well as that of Attakullakulla and the people of Chota. When reprisals came in the form of Colonel William Christian and the Virginia-Western Carolina Army, Nancy Ward and the people of Chota were treated as neutrals. While the crops of other Cherokee villages were destroyed in the fields and the winter corn burned, the people of Chota were spared. Christian listened to the Ghighau's plea on behalf of the peaceable villages, and said, "I will distinguish between those towns which have behaved well toward us, and those which have not." He kept his word. Dragging Canoe moved further west to Chickamauga, and the Americans put a price on his head.

Alliances remained confused. The Cherokees had always been puzzled by the war between the English and the Americans. "Why are these people who speak the same language at war?" they asked. Now, the English and the Americans found themselves subject to the same confusion. Which village has an alliance with the English? Which is neutral? Which has "raised the war axe with Dragging Canoe?" It was often the Ghighau who sorted them out. Again and again, she stepped forward at a critical moment. Settlers bartering for corn found themselves surrounded by angry Cherokees shouting, "Why should we trade with you? That gun you carry has been used to kill Cherokee warriors." Suddenly the Ghinghau would appear, soothing hot tempers, repeating over and over her favorite litany: "We must learn to live together. It is our only hope."

The Revolutionary War dragged on. By 1780, the English were losing ground throughout the Carolinas. When Nancy Ward heard that John Sevier's troops had dwindling provisions, she sent a small herd of cattle. No doubt this was a wise and calculated move, executed to remind Sevier that she was a friend. Her daughter married Colonel Joseph Martin, noted American officer, and the alliance became stronger. Time and time again she asked the Americans to spare hostile villages. Spare Hiawassee and Chestua, she said. There are many Cherokees living there who do not support the war against the Americans. She was not always successful, but the officers always listened respectfully.

When violence broke out near Chota, the Americans moved the Ghighau and her family to Long Island on the Holston. On July 26, 1781, a delegation of Cherokee chiefs came to Long Island to discuss treaty terms with the Americans. Nancy Ward came with a delegation of women and sat quietly listening to the treaty talk. There were many grievances on both sides, and old wounds rankled. Amid the charges and counter-charges, the Ghighau stood. She said she knew that warriors looked upon women as nothing when it came to warfare, but "...we are your mothers; you are our sons. OUR CRY IS ALL FOR PEACE." Both Cherokees and whites were quiet. Then, Colonel Christian spoke directly to the Ghighau and the assembly of mothers. Very well, he said, the women are right. We are all descendants of the same mother after all, so let us live in peace.

132

The treaty was signed. The war was almost over, but skirmishes flared throughout eastern Tennessee. Dragging Canoe had signed no treaties. The Ghighau and the old chief, Oconostota, sought refuge with her daughter Nancy and Nancy's husband Joseph Martin among the Wataugans. In the spring of 1783, the old chief, sensing the approach of death, asked to be taken back to Chota. Shortly afterwards, he died, and Joseph Martin buried him in a dugout canoe near "The Mother Town." Nancy Ward returned to her home and found the countryside filled with victims of war: homeless children, women and orphaned half-breeds. The war was over, but the homeless were everywhere. The Ghighau's home became a refuge.

The years following the Paris Peace Treaty, which officially ended the American Revolution, were difficult ones for Nancy Ward. At first, it appeared that the Hopewell Treaty, which acknowledged the Cherokee's rights to the much disputed lands between the Cumberland River and the Nolichucky, would honor the rights of the Cherokees. Five thousand settlers were ordered out of eastern Tennessee. No doubt the government had good intentions, but the conditions were impossible to enforce. The settlers would not leave, and more arrived each day.

Gradually, the Cherokee warriors began to drift towards Chickamauga and Dragging Canoe. Chota was soon deserted except for the women and children. "Is it not as I told you?" asked Dragging Canoe. "You cannot trust the white man's treaty. We must take our land back with the knife and gun."

Bloody fighting broke out again. Clashes between John Sevier and the Cherokees became increasingly brutal. Five Cherokee chiefs were murdered under a flag of truce, and Sevier killed 145 Cherokee warriors in a cul-de-sac on Flint Creek. At Chota, the Ghighau found that Cherokee leaders no longer sought her council. Another treaty was drawn at Holston, and the Cherokees were forced to relinquish all the country "between the forks of the Holston and the French Broad." Then, after developing plans for acquiring allies from the Creeks and the Choctaws, Dragging Canoe died on March 1, 1792. Many of his associates felt that the sixty-year-old war chief had died of exhaustion. For all intents and purposes, significant resistance to the continued encroachment of white settlers died with him.

And what of Nancy Ward? She is quiet now. She gathers her family about her, tends her cattle and visits her grandchildren. One story relates how the Ghighau went on a journey to the Tugaloo River in South Carolina where Bryant Ward lived. Here is a mystery. Did Nancy Ward still love that Irishman who had once served in the English army? Is it possible that Nancy smuggled him out of Chota so he would not fall victim to a reprisal from the Americans? That is certainly one interpretation of her visit. And she returned again on several occasions before her death.

She did deliver one more message. In 1818, word reached her that the federal government had offered the Cherokees large tracts of land beyond the Mississippi if they would sign papers indicating that they gave up any claim to land in Tennessee and Georgia. She had heard that some Cherokees were tempted to accept. So it was that the Ghighau spoke for the last time. Unable to attend in person because of her age, she sent a letter by her son Five Killer, and she asked that he be allowed to vote on any measures before the Council. Further, she said that she had sent her walking stick to the Council, and all who knew her would recognize it. Instead of the legendary swan's wing, Five Killer had been told to hold her walking stick aloft to indicate her vote.

The Ghighau urged her children to reject the "paper talk." Stay where you belong, she said. This is your country, and you must not leave it. The message in the letter repeated her favorite themes. Learn to farm. Accept the white man's world. Give your children the security of a home in a country that has always been occupied by Cherokees. "Listen," she said, "I have great-grandchildren ... I wish them to do well on our land."

Not long afterwards, when the Cherokees were told that they could acquire reservation grants for unsettled tracts of land in Tennessee, Nancy Ward applied. Specifically, she asked for "a section of land one mile below

John McIntosh's on Mouse Creek where the Old Trace crosses said creek leading into Tellico Blockhouse to Hiawassee Garrison." She further noted that henceforth, she would live as a citizen of the United States. Her application was rejected.

So, what are we to make of this woman? Did she betray her people or did she save them? Pat Alderman, the Tennessee historian who has written much about the Ghighau, maintains that she was a fighter for human rights, not a traitor to her people.

Nancy Ward died in the spring of 1824. John Walker Hildebrand, Nancy Ward's great-grandson, was four years old when he walked with the Ghighau's descendants to the graveyard. Blessed with a remarkable memory, Hildebrand afterwards told how he walked with his father along the "old war path"... past Five Killer's cabin, crossing the Oconee at Woman Killer Ford, then along the war path up a little valley...up a hill to an open grave. He was puzzled by the large number of cooking utensils in the grave until he was told that his great-grandmother would use them in the next world.

But this is not Hildebrand's most remarkable memory. Knowing that many people would not believe the story, he signed a sworn statement about what happened at the moment that "Granny Ward" died. Hildebrand said that he was standing in the room when she drew her final breath, and then "A light rose from her body, fluttered around the room like a bird, left through an open door and disappeared toward Chota."

Those who knew Nancy Ward and of her love for the "Mother Town," were inclined to believe him.

The Ghighau had gone home.

G.C.

135

HONEST JOHN
KING OF THE ROGUE BEARS

One-hundred years ago, bears and bear hunters often acquired celebrity status. Mountaineers such as Quill Rose, "Big Tom" Wilson and "Uncle Fed" Medford were celebrated for their kills, frequently claiming records in the hundreds. As a matter of integrity, the hunters made a distinction between the bears that they had killed single-handed, and the kills in which they had merely participated.

In all instances, since the ferocity and stature of the animal enhanced the hunter's reputation, everyone had a yarn about a legendary bruin who was uncommonly intelligent, huge...and maimed. Names such as "Reelfoot," "Fiddlefoot" or "One-eared Joe" are examples of legendary bears who had either been caught in a trap, escaped and were henceforth identified by a mangled footprint or a missing eye or ear which had been lost in hand-to-paw combat with an erstwhile hunter, usually the one who will one day bring the bear's reign of terror to an end. Invariably, the bears live to be old warriors, and it is not uncommon to read accounts of marauding bears who are fifty or sixty years old. However, we still do not have a celebrity bear unless he has a reputation for being a flesh-eater.

Unlike his brothers and sisters who are vegetarians except for an occasional fish or injured raccoon, the rogue bear has tasted flesh, usually pork, and liked it so much he decides to make it his primary food.

Now, we need only add a touch of the supernatural ("Thet bear knows who is huntin' him 'n how many."); a bit of notoriety ("He's been terrorizing this section for fifteen years!"); and a vendetta ("Me 'n him, we got a score to settle!"). In effect, the bear acquires the qualities of a murderous bandit. A posse is sent out to bring him to justice and the hunt acquires dramatic trappings. "This is a duel to the death!" says the hunter. "I respect old Fiddlefoot 'cause he is brave, but he has done gone too fer. He's got to pay!"

Time after time, the old bear turned in some mountain vale or atop a rocky crest and fought his last fight. Accounts of the final battle are replete with the death of faithful hounds ("He broke Old Bob's back 'n throwed him in the river. Thet's when I said 'Today ye die!'"). The triumphant return of the "posse" with the dead bear was usually anti-climactic. Somehow, the mangled corpse, bear or man, of a deadly killer never seems to inspire either respect or fear. ("Don't look so tough now, does he?")

By the 1930's, notorious killer bears were definitely on the decline. Ironically, that seems to be the very reason an occasional report of a slaughtered hog would be carried in regional newspapers and gun-wielding mountain men would unleash the dogs and rush into the diminishing wilderness eager for one more encounter with a rogue bear.

During the winter of 1934, reports began to circulate that "Honest John" was terrorizing the counties of Jackson and Haywood in western North Carolina. How did he get his name? "Well, he ain't like other maverick bears," said a native of the Caney Fork community. "When he visits your pig lot, he don't kill every pig. He just picks one up and runs back up the mountain with it under his arm." To many newspapers in the region, this sounded like a prelude to a duel that pitted keen-eyed mountain men against a brutal, pork-loving beast.

City journalists began to appear.

"Have you ever heard of Honest John?"

"You mean that hog-killer? Shore have. He's been killing hogs 'round here for over twenty years."

"How old is he?"

"Well, you have to ask Wilburn Parker about that. He is King of the Bear Hunters in these parts. I think he knows more 'bout that bear than anybody."

The journalists found Parker on his Caney Fork farm. The newspapermen watched Wilburn feed his Plott hounds.

"Sir, how many bears have you killed?"

"Fifty-four. Thet's me, by myself. Now, I participated with others in one-hundred and sixteen. I aim to get a even hundred 'fore I quit. Jest me by myself."

"Tell me about Honest John."

"I know him. He knows me, too."

"How old would you say he is?"

"Between fifty and sixty. Thet's pretty old fer a bear. Most of 'em stop a bullet by the time they are three or four."

"How do you account for him being so old?"

"He's smart. Runs circles 'round most dogs. If things git hot, he cuts out for Haywood County. Crosses the Balsams. Hides in the laurel hells and rhododendron thickets over in the Plott Balsams."

"How do you know the difference between a hog killed by Honest John and some other bear? Maybe you are giving him credit for what a lot of bears are doing."

"Nope. He allus leaves his track like he was proud of what he done. Part of his left forepaw is missing. Thet happened near twenty years ago, when he got in one of my traps. Thet bear jest took thet trap and frailed it aginst a big rock 'till it come off. We tracked 'em by the blood a good ways, but he got away. Went back to Haywood County.

"Nother thang. Thet track is the biggest I ever saw. Looks like it was left by one of them prehistoric monsters. You can put a ordinary hat over it 'n it won't cover it from heel to toe." Parker hesitated, then he said, "Them hogs he kills are mostly razorbacks, 'n a razorback in these parts is jest 'bout as dangerous as a bear. Hit ain't lak a tame hog out in the lot. 'Course, mountain folks, they claim they own herds of razorbacks jest lak they was in the lot. Honest John jest comes to the pig lot when he can't find a razorback."

The journalists were impressed. They scribbled for a while, and then one asked, "How come you never killed him?"

"I tried a time or two. Couldn't git close enough. Seen him lots of times jest 'fore he disappeared down the backside of a ridge half a mile away. He'd allus stand up on his hind legs and look back at me. He's over six feet tall and weighs in the neighborhood of seven-hundred pounds. Tell ye the truth, I kinda like him. But, lately, he's been getting out of hand. Killed lots of hogs the last two years. Guess I'm gonna have to put a stop to it." Parker sounded reluctant.

"Mr. Parker, do you mind if I say you have "eyes of steel?" Parker stared at the reporter.

"It's just a descriptive phrase, sir. I would like to say that you are pursuing Honest John with cold determination and that when you stare towards the snow-covered Balsams where the fiendish killer lives, your eyes had the chilly glint of blue steel."

Parker smiled like a man who had heard a child say something comical. "Whatever gives you pleasure," he said.

"When are you going after him?"

"Well, the bear-hunting season don't close 'til January 16th. I've got plenty of time."

Several days later, heavy snows blanketed the Balsams. An accumulation of two feet quickly turned into four-foot drifts in the wind-swept hollows of Caney Fork. Temperatures dropped, and the wind hooted and wailed in the high reaches of Plott Mountain. "Not a fit night for man or beast," said the old-timers. They were wrong.

On successive nights the squeals of doomed pigs woke families in Caney Fork and Tuckaseegee. Men struggled through the wind and dark to find themselves bereft of a sow or boar, always the biggest of the brood. Each time, the trampled snow in the pig lot was branded by the huge, distinctive footprint. Honest John was back.

The reporter from the Asheville *Citizen* found Parker with a dozen hunters who sat quietly as the King of the Bear Hunters responded to questions.

"Why haven't you gone after him?"

"A man would be a fool to go out in thet wind and snow. Dogs can't travel through four-foot drifts. Honest John knows thet. We'll wait 'til it thaws. We've done decided thet the only way to git him is to "'slow track'" him."

"Slow track?" The reporter's pencil was poised.

"The reason nobody ever catches him is they charge off at a run atter him, and by the time they catch up, the dogs are all wore out, no fight in them. Ole John, he jest slaps them down and goes on 'bout his business. We aim to take our time, 'n if we see him, we ain't gonna lose our heads. Jest take it easy, so if we ever do catch up with him, we'll all be rested and ready fer a fight. I jest need one shot."

"So, is that a fool-proof plan?"

"No, it ain't. If ole John figures out what we're doing, hit ain't worth doodly-squat."

Three days later, Parker, his cohorts and a dozen dogs set out to bring Honest John to justice. He had declared the killer bear Public Enemy No. 1 and had vowed to bring him in. For several days and nights, the residents of Caney Fork and Tuckasegee heard the baying of hounds in the far reaches of the Balsams.

When Parker came out of the woods several days later, the *Citizen* reporter was waiting. He looked for the trophy, the slaughtered bruin lashed to a hickory pole, his hide torn by the dogs.

No bear. Men and dogs seemed subdued. Parker's posse quietly dispersed towards home, leaving Wilburn to deal with the disappointed journalist.

"Did you see him?"

"Once." Wilburn was tired. He stared at the fog-wrapped Balsams. "We was climbing towards the Haywood County line when we seen him. He was on a bluff 'cross this ravine. He was 'bout fifty yards away, but it might as well a-been a mile or two. Dogs went crazy 'cause they cou'nt git near him. He stood up like he allus did, reared up 'n looked at us." Wilburn shook his head. "Thet bear was old. Ears all tore up 'n ragged, hide turning gray. He looked at us fer a good while 'n we looked at him. Then, he was gone."

"Did you shoot at him? Seems he was close enough."

Parker shook his head. "How old ye think I am?" he said.

The reporter, confused by the change of subject, looked at Parker.

"I believe ye said in your paper thet 'the white hair on my head testified to the passage of sixty winters.' Well, thet bear has been around about the same amount of time, 'n we're both beginning to feel our age."

The reporter was astonished. "Are you saying you let him go?"

"I didn't say that. Said we was both tired."

"Are you going back?"

Parker shook his head. "I'll go bear hunting again, but it won't be fer Honest John. I hear there's a bunch of hunters over in Haywood thet are going atter him."

"What am I supposed to put in the paper? I mean, after the big build-up, we don't have an ending, or at least not the ending that the readers expect."

Parker thought a minute. "Why don't you say he got away. Why don't ye say that tonight he is asleep in a cave somewhere atop the Plott Balsams surrounded by laurel hells ... which is what I'd like to do, sleep." Parker turned towards his home. He seemed to hesitate for a moment and then turned to the reporter.

"How did it go again, what ye put in the paper 'bout my eyes... 'the cold glint of blue steel'?"

"I said that when you looked toward the Balsams, your eyes had 'the chilly glint of blue steel.'"

"That's it!" Wilburn nodded and smiled. He turned away, chuckling, and the reporter heard him repeating the phrase, "the chilly glint of blue steel" as he walked away.

Several weeks later, John Holzworth arrived. When word spread that Mr. Holzworth, accompanied by a one-hundred-thirty-pound Great Dane named Ajax, was interviewing anyone who had ever seen Honest John, the newspapers talked to him. The visitor was the Chairman of the Alaska Bear Committee and the New York Zoological Society. He was also a noted author and authority on the behavior of bears.

"Why are you interested in Honest John?"

"Well, he is a famous bear. His reputation has spread to New York and Alaska, and based on my interviews thus far, he has remarkable survival instincts."

"Do you intend to hunt him down?"

Holzworth was amused. "Heavens, no! I would no more harm Honest John than I would Ajax, here." Holzworth gave his dog an affectionate pat. "But I would like to take his picture."

Several weeks later, Holzworth appeared again. He announced that Honest John would be a chapter in a book he was writing, and he was eager to talk to hunters who had seen the giant bear. He interviewed hunters in Haywood County, journeyed to Sunburst where the bear had been repeatedly sighted, and was finally told about Wilburn Parker.

"Where is he?" asked Holzworth.

A resident of Sunburst pointed vaguely toward the Balsams.

"He lives the back side of beyond," he said. "Go down to the forks of the Pigeon 'n go up thet little holler to the left." Parker and his wife greeted Holzworth with mountain hospitality, and the weathered hunter talked about the Terror of the Balsams.

"Will you be going after him again?" asked Holzworth.

"Maybe, maybe not. Seems like half the hunters in the mountains are going atter 'em."

And so they did. After a half-dozen trips, a Jackson County hunting club wrote the state game commissioner for permission to hunt Honest John out of season. They argued that he had become a significant threat and should be killed. The answer was not what they expected. John D. Chalk, North Carolina's game commissioner, warned all hunters in the Great Smoky Mountains Park area that the bear known as Honest John was an inhabitant of the Park and thereby subject to the Park's protection. Sportsmen in Haywood County wrote Chalk, applauding his action. Most letters noted that the old bear was not the notorious killer he had been made out to be; in fact, he was highly respected in Haywood County.

And so, the posses halted. As the winter dragged on, and no further reports of Honest John appeared, one editor of a local paper, noted for his wit, observed that perhaps Honest John had eaten so much raw pork he had succumbed to trichinosis.

Reports of raids by Honest John continued until 1942. He was "killed" a dozen times, but invariably the dead bear lacked Honest John's distinguishing characteristics. However, a giant bear killed near Cullowhee in the winter of 1942 was widely reported to be the ancient bruin. "Shore was a big 'n," said the man who killed him, "but I jest don't know." The old bear was never reported again. Was he dead? Perhaps.

Or perhaps, for many years, as Parker said, he slept the winters away, and finally changed his diet to berries, honey and mast, slept in the sun and died of old age. Perhaps his skull lies moldering in a rhododendron thicket somewhere in the Balsams — all that remains of the rogue bear that got away.

G.C.

PART IV

FACTS STRANGER
THAN FICTION

THE LAST BATTLE

The last fighting of the Civil War in North Carolina occurred in the mountains. The last Civil War soldier to die during the state's conflict is buried in the mountains, and all things considered, the final chapter of the war is a strange story made almost bizarre because the winning side was allowed to surrender.

Even though General Lee had surrendered Confederate forces at Appomattox, fighting continued in remote areas, especially in the westernmost mountains of North Carolina. Union officers Bartlett and Kirk were ordered into the hills to stop the guerrillas.

There had not been a major battle fought in the region, but Kirk and his raiders were known and hated. Earlier in the war, Kirk had plundered and killed without reason throughout the mountains, doing it all in the name of military necessity.

He must have felt he owned the mountains because he led his soldiers through the valleys and across the ridges at such speed he quickly outdistanced his companion, Bartlett. Bartlett was unaware Kirk's zeal had put him so far ahead; Bartlett always assumed Kirk was nearby and close enough to help. That was his first mistake.

Bartlett's second mistake was deciding to make Waynesville his headquarters. The Union force had taken the hamlet of fifteen or twenty houses without a shot. Tired of war, the soldiers selected a campsite on the Love estate where it was quiet, restful and offered the pleasures of a spring

147

with a slightly medicinal smell, just the kind of place lowlanders had been visiting for their health. The camp promised a day or two of basking in the healing waters and enjoying the scenery.

The soldiers certainly deserved a rest. Why had they been chosen for another fight when the war was over, and everyone else was at home? It's easy to understand why the Union soldiers selected the site, but Waynesville lies on a mountain plateau surrounded by mountain ranges. The soldiers were in a position not unlike that of defending the bottom of a bowl. Control of the mountain tops was militarily important, which both sides understood, but, oh, how those soldiers must have wanted a rest.

Of course, mountain residents knew all about the Union force. Word of their movements had preceded them, and Confederate Colonel William Holland Thomas knew what to do about the Union presence. Thomas' Legion was composed of Cherokee and white soldiers who had seen duty outside the mountains during the early months of the war, but the unit had been back in the mountains for quite some time when Bartlett and Kirk came. Fiercely committed to their mountain homes, members of the Thomas Legion resented the Union invasion.

Colonel Thomas ordered Private Rice into civilian clothes. He told the young soldier to gather all the information he could about the Yankees and to stay in town long enough to do some talking of his own. Rice was to talk about the Thomas Legion and to give exaggerated numbers about the size of the unit.

Rice headed for Waynesville and began spreading tall tales while Colonel Thomas moved sharp shooters to the mountain tops. He also sent a small company of Confederates into the woods surrounding the sulphur springs.

Quite by accident, the Confederates ran right into the enemy at the springs. There was fighting and a Union soldier named Arwood was killed. At his death, Arwood earned the distinction of being the last man killed in the state's Civil War action. He was buried near Asheville, N.C.

The skirmish and Arwood's death caught the Union soldiers off guard. Many fled. Those who remained were disoriented. None of this was supposed to be happening. The war was over. Didn't these mountain Confederates know that?

Colonel Bartlett was alarmed. He was hearing stories about the size of the Thomas Legion, and the numbers were much larger than he expected. His scouts reported Confederate soldiers moving in from the south and the west. Bartlett would have been even more worried if he'd known about the soldiers climbing to the top of Rocky Knob and Old Field Top high above Waynesville. Dusk was near when Bartlett sent a messenger to Kirk requesting help.

Kirk, racing ahead, had put far too many miles between his troops and Bartlett's to return in time to help. And as darkness overtook the mountain town, the Union soldiers started counting campfires on the surrounding mountainsides. Hundreds of fires glowed on all four sides. How many Johnny Rebs could there be?

Then the night air was jarred by sudden warwhoops and chilling screams. And just when the soldiers were getting accustomed to the frightening sounds, the drums started. All night long the soldiers were forced to listen to the rhythms of Cherokee preparations for battle. It was a long, sleepless night.

In the morning, Bartlett sent out a flag of truce. In response, Colonel Thomas appeared, accompanied by twenty fierce looking Cherokees in full war paint and feathers. These were Colonel Thomas' friends, not Confederate soldiers, but Bartlett did not know that.

Neither did he know that the night before had been a beautifully orchestrated bit of psychological warfare. Thomas had sent his men across the mountains to build fires. There were far more campfires than soldiers the prior night, and Cherokee members of the Legion added to the drama by making the hideous screams. Neither was there a war dance, just Cherokee soldiers spooking the enemy.

149

In truth, the Thomas Legion was out-numbered, and any serious fighting would have found the mountaineers at a disadvantage. But Colonel Thomas kept up the charade as he approached Bartlett. A normally cool, aloof man, Thomas was quite boisterous, even aggressive, that morning. He demanded that Bartlett's men stop stealing horses, cows and oxen. If the thievery did not stop at once, Thomas swore to turn his Indians loose on the regiment and have every last soldier scalped.

The threat and strangely dressed soldiers after the fearsome night were enough for Bartlett to request that further talks be held in some place more to his understanding, a nearby tourist hotel.

Undeniably, the Confederates had won, but what were the two sides to do? A Union surrender would simply bring in more Union soldiers, and then the mountain Confederates would truly have problems. Negotiations went on for several days. In the end, the mountaineers decided in favor of surrender if Bartlett and Kirk would stop plundering and leave the countryside and if Confederate soldiers could keep their guns and ammunition.

Union higher-ups balked at the mountain soldiers' keeping guns, so talks stalled, but it really didn't matter much. Soldiers on both sides were leaving daily. Most simply walked off, heading back to their farms. When an agreement was reached it officially marked the last skirmish of the Civil War in North Carolina as ending on May 9, 1865, one month after Lee's surrender.

Years later, one of the soldiers present at the mountain conclusion to the Civil War said, "I say surrender, but the better word would be quit, for I don't think we really ever did surrender. In fact, we just disbanded and carried our guns and cartridges home with us."

N.A.

THE UNDYING FIRE

William Morris thought Hamp Alexander Owens had stopped to talk a spell, but after settling into the comfortable split-bottom chair of the Saluda, N.C., cabin, Owens said, "I've come to tell you that I'll keep your fire going."

The words were a relief for William. He had spent considerable time and effort worrying about the family fire during the last few years. The fire in his hearth at that moment was one originally ignited more than one-hundred-fifty years earlier, and now the old man knew the fire would continue burning after he was dead.

When William Morris was born in 1860, the fire was more than eighty years old. As a child he hadn't been impressed as his parents checked the fire daily and used it as a reason to recite family history.

"Robert Morris was your great-great-uncle," they said. "He was a signer of the Declaration of Independence and a delegate to the Continental Congress of 1775. Later he donated large sums of money to help support the Thirteen Colonies. There are people who say he saved the young nation at an important time."

That ancestor owned considerable land in North Carolina, more than seventy-thousand acres according to one account, but it was John Morris, Robert's brother and William's great-great-grandfather, who first settled in the state near Rutherfordton.

"This fire was started with flint and steel when your great-great-grandfather first built his house," William's parents said, and when the family moved from the original Morris dwelling into their own home a mile away, coals from the fire were carried to the new cabin.

The admonition, "The fire must never be allowed to go out," required considerable attention during William's childhood since matches were rare and expensive. Of course, there were other family heirlooms with attached histories — the Yankee sword from the Civil War, grandmother Ward's 1829 Bible, an old piece of Indian pottery, a Kentucky rifle — all were important, but keeping the Morris fire burning was the most important.

Although he never married or had children, William dutifully repeated all the family history to nieces and nephews, cared for the family treasures and kept the fire burning. By the time he was seventy-seven, he had become a dignified, courtly mountain gentleman not the least bit hesitant to tell people that the fire he maintained was now one-hundred-fifty years old. Eventually a reporter for the *Spartanburg Herald* heard the story and visited the old man.

After the newspaper article about William and his fire appeared, he received a letter from the Phillips Lord Studio in New York. William's fire seemed perfect for the "We-the-People" program heard over the National Broadcasting Company, and he was asked to come to New York City for a broadcast, which he agreed to only after he made arrangements for care of the fire.

"Well, after that radio program I heard from Morrises from practically every state in the Union," he said. It was an amazement and possibly a solution.

"I worry sometimes that there is no one to keep the fire burning when I'm gone," he said. "It would give me great satisfaction to know that it would never die down, but since none of my family are interested, I fear the fire will go out with me when I die."

William's request for a caretaker of the fire was carried in newspapers across North Carolina. *The State* magazine ran an article, and there was a small movement to have the National Park Service move him, his cabin and all the surrounding buildings to park land where he could live out his life.

After his death, the fire would be maintained and his cabin and out buildings would become a sort of pioneer homestead display. The plan did not materialize, but it was of no consequence after Hamp Owens volunteered to become the tender of the fire.

William Morris died knowing that the fire, now called "the Saluda fire," would continue to burn. In 1948, Owens died, and while he undoubtedly accomplished other things during his life, the notice of his death identified him as "the keeper of the Saluda fire." By this time the continuous fire was well past one-hundred-seventy years old.

What became of the fire is unclear. At Owens' death a newspaper article stated that at least one National Park Service administrator was checking into ways the fire could be kept burning, but there is no follow-up article about what did happen. In Polk County, William Morris and his fire remain quite famous. Various histories of the county tell the story of the hearthfire's long life but none describe what became of it, and one historian finds the chief value of the story "is its historical significance as evidence bearing on the type of citizens who were the first settlers."

That may be, but then every local history would like to claim only the finest citizenry. Perhaps more important is the dedication and concern William Morris and his ancestors felt for this fire. It was a symbol of the eternal human quest for independence and freedom and a reminder that the sparks of freedom need to be continuously and carefully tended. Too bad we don't know what became of that glow of patriotic diligence.

It is possible the Saluda Fire continues to burn. Scores of people still remember its story, so perhaps it is smoldering still, banked in some fireplace waiting to be fanned into full flame.

Where might it be? Quietly tended by whom? Does the present caretaker have the same concerns William Morris had about future arrangements for the fire? Or have we passed into an age when such things are mere foolishness?

N.A.

Memorial to Joe on the campus of Mars Hill College

SOLD FOR A COLLEGE EDUCATION

Mrs. Carter never wanted to send Melvin off to the Burnsville Academy in the first place. "He's only twelve," she said, "and small for his age. Why do we have to send him off? Why can't you start a school closer to home?" Of course, her objections were ignored by her husband, Edward Carter, and Melvin, along with his cousins, Polly and Mack Ray, was shipped off to the only school anywhere near the families' mountain homes.

In the 1850s there weren't many choices, and the Burnsville Academy was where parents who found education worthwhile sent their children.

But now Edward Carter was upset. He had just been told that while at the Burnsville school, Mack and Polly had converted to the Methodist Church. Melvin had not embraced Methodism, but perhaps he might during the next revival; after all, the academy was a Methodist school. What was a good Baptist father to do? He sent his oldest son off to get a good education, but did that mean the boy might forsake the Baptist faith?

Mr. Carter undoubtedly recalled his wife's suggestion as he worried about the plight of mountain Baptists for several days. During this time he had to attend court at Burnsville where he happened upon Nathan Young, a prominent Baptist from Rutherfordton. When he explained his concerns to Young and mentioned the notion of establishing a school for Baptist children, Mr. Young was encouraging.

"Make sure you gather some support from other Baptists and then have a paper drawn up obligating each person who signs to pay so much cash as he indicates next to his name. Write out that the purpose of the paper is for building such a school."

Carter asked, "Could you write up the paper?"

"Surely." And Young promptly did so.

Edward Carter returned to his mountain farm and began spending part of each day visiting his neighbors. When he presented the paper each person saw that the first signature was Edward Carter's with the pledge of one-hundred dollars next to his name. Reverend J.W. Anderson was the second signer, and he subscribed for fifty dollars. Encouraged, Mr. Carter approached Reverend Keith.

"Well, I don't know about this," said Reverend Keith. "This paper doesn't say where the college will be located. And there are folks over at Ivey who have been talking about a school there. Where would this school of yours be?"

Reverend Keith may have thought his statement would send Carter away for a few days. Instead, Carter stood up and replied, "Well, since you've raised the question, let's settle it right now," and he headed for the door.

Keith was obliged to follow. Carter picked up a stake and proceeded to walk toward his own property where on a rolling knoll he put the marker in the ground and drove it down firmly. "How about right here?" he asked.

Reverend Keith signed the paper and subscribed for fifty dollars. Carter's campaign continued until he had raised two-thousand dollars, then he went to contractors in Asheville. and ordered bricks made and lumber sawed. Construction of the first building was begun right at the place where Carter had driven his stake.

When the work was completed, the contractors were not paid in full. There remained a debt of about $1100. Who was going to pay the remaining debt? The signers could divide the debt, each paying a portion, but no one rushed to do that, and the contractor began looking for ways to collect.

Although the men who signed the school document were considered well-off, most were wealthy only in terms of land. No one had a thousand dollars in cash, and few owned any one item worth that much. Most trade was done either through barter or credit; actual money was rare. As the contractor considered ways of collecting, he learned that signer J.W. Anderson owned a strong, healthy young Negro slave named Joe, a possession certainly worth the debt.

Without any warning, Joe was seized and taken to the Asheville jail in payment of the debt. News of Joe's imprisonment spread quickly, in part because Joe was a pleasant man known and liked throughout the community. No one liked the idea of Joe sitting in jail because of the school's debt.

Joe's imprisonment became a legal judgment against the school's president and secretary of the board of trustees, T.W. Ray and J.W. Anderson. The two men convened the other signers of the school document and together met in the newly built east room of the school "with their faces in their hands" and agreed to share the burden between them.

Within a few days the bill was paid and Joe released. The legend that has grown around Joe's incarceration is based on the fact that as far as anyone can remember it was the only instance in which a human being was taken to secure payment for a school which would become a college, Mars Hill College. In the 1920's the story was revived and sent to Ripley's "Believe It or Not." At the college, the incident is often referred to as a symbol of the human values that went into the college's founding.

One variation of the legend is that Joe volunteered to become the security deposit for the school's debt, but the truth of that is unknown. After the Civil War, J.W. Anderson gave Joe a parcel of land, southwest of the small college, which upon Joe's death returned to the Anderson family. Joe lived his life out in the small village, doing odd jobs, but the exact date of his death is unclear, sometime between 1900 and 1910. He was buried in a private cemetery on a nearby farm with graves of other former slaves. In 1932, permission was received to open Joe's grave and bury him near the south

157

entrance of Mars Hill College. On Founders' Day, October 12 of that year, a ceremony was held to unveil the granite marker of Joe's grave. The marker and stone steps leading to the memorial still stand.

IN MEMORY OF

JOE

A SLAVE WHO WAS TAKEN

BY THE CONTRACTORS OF

THE FIRST BUILDING OF

THIS COLLEGE AS A PLEDGE

FOR THE DEBT DUE THEM

1936

Time moved on, once again presenting what appears to be a pattern for life. The little school grew, added more buildings, expanded curricula, proudly presented the first collegiate baseball team in the North Carolina mountains, and in September 1961, admitted Oralene Graves as the first African-American student to enroll at the college as a full-time resident student. Oralene Graves was Joe's great-great-granddaughter.

N.A.

YOU GOT IT, DIDN'T YOU?

The request for a doctor did not thrill Dr. J. Howell Way of Waynesville, N.C. Not in January of 1902 as snow flurries promised more miserable weather. And, of course, the patient lived way out in the mountains, somewhere close to the highest point in the Balsam Range.

Dr. Way probably never described himself as a good ol' country doctor, and he wasn't. He'd earned a medical degree from Vanderbilt University in a time when most physicians simply "read medicine" and then passed a state licensing exam. A man with a strong intellect, a superior education and a confidence close to arrogance, Dr. Way had originally come to the hamlet of Waynesville with the intention of leaving soon. He'd planned to make some money, expand his medical library, invest in some good medical equipment and head for a place where a smart physician could make a reliable income. Mountain families had little ready cash.

But then he'd married and developed friendships, and soon he was a respected, if not well paid, physician in a growing mountain community. Dr. Way's reputation was probably the reason the tough logger had sent for him.

To get to his patient, Dr. Way had to ride the train for two hours and then walk a mile over snowy paths to the patient's home. Later, when Dr. Way wrote of his experience in a medical journal, he described the patient as a "stout, sturdy mountaineer, aged 22, weighing 168 pounds." The man's pulse was ninety, temperature 101.4, and Dr. Way observed that the "tongue was a trifle coated."

The patient could not talk clearly; his speech was slurred, but Dr. Way guessed at words as the patient nodded either yes or no, and the two men used hand gestures to communicate. Slowly, the doctor pieced together the story.

About eight days earlier, the logger and some friends had taken "Christmas in a way spiritual, but not proper," and the patient had received some lacerations and a blow to the head. Dr. Way could see a slight scalp wound about one-half-inch long, and there was a cut on the upper lip. The logger was not concerned about his scalp because it had healed, but the moment the physician touched the lip wound, the patient was thrown into a convulsion that lasted about forty seconds.

Dr. Way noticed the "spasm was limited to the right side of the body only, and a more careful study of the convulsive movements, which were readily excited by slight handling of the upper lip, showed the spasm to be limited to the muscles of the right forearm and leg." The tongue, when protruded, showed an inclination to the right side, but the patient's mental condition seemed normal, so Dr. Way continued to look for an answer as to why the man's speech was suddenly slurred and why the convulsions.

As he examined the scalp wound, he noticed swelling but "no evidence of a fractured skull." Perhaps it was some intracranial lesion inducing the convulsions. The doctor decided to have a look. With the light from a small kerosene lamp and one lantern and the assistance of a man who was a farmer and bear hunter of some local repute, Dr. Way administered chloroform to the patient and opened the scalp wound.

"A long curvilinear flap with the wound in its center was dissected and turned down," wrote Dr. Way. "...The skull being bare, the same straight smooth cut, as noted on the scalp, was seen to enter the skull, but there was no evidence of any foreign body in the cut to the skull bone." Dr. Way removed "a button of the bone" and once again found nothing. He was beginning to be perplexed.

For no definite reason, except maybe curiosity, he put his index finger "within the opening and moved backward beneath the cut in the skull." There he discovered the "big blade of the ordinary farmer's pocket knife ... exactly one and five-eighths of an inch in length."

At the moment Dr. Way withdrew the blade from the patient's head, the logger, who was anaesthetized, spoke quite clearly and distinctly. "Doc, you got it, didn't you?"

The patient suffered no hemorrhaging or adverse reaction to the anesthetic. Within two months he returned to full-time work at the logging camp. Dr. Way remained in Waynesville, serving several terms as president of the North Carolina Medical Society and as a member of the State Board of Health.

N.A.

FOR AN OLD GRAY MARE

Shortly after the turn of the twentieth century, North Carolina Congressman Edward Pou was comfortably arranged behind his Washington, D.C., desk, reading *The Smithfield Herald*, his hometown newspaper. A fellow Congressman from Arkansas walked into the office and said, "Ah, Smithfield's your town home?"

"Yes," replied Pou.

"I've got a neighbor out in Arkansas who came from Smithfield."

"What's his name?" asked Pou.

"John Jones" was the reply.

After more questioning, Congressman Pou was convinced that the Arkansas John Jones was related to a family he knew, and the family had been looking for John for quite some time.

Originally there had been ten children in the Jones family, and it was John who left home to seek his fortune in the West. The family never heard from him. By the time the father died, only three children were left — Catherine, William and Burkett. The father's will left his estate to the three children with the stipulation that if the missing John was ever located, he was to share equally.

When Congressman Pou returned to Smithfield, he went to see Burkett Jones and explained what he had been told about John Jones and said he believed the Arkansas Jones was the missing brother. Burkett listened, but he wasn't sure. How many John Joneses could there be? Probably a great many who weren't given that name by parents from North Carolina. Sure didn't seem like much to go on, but Burkett did write to his brother, William, in Paris, Tennessee.

William, a Baptist minister, thought they should at least get in touch with the Arkansas man, so several letters were exchanged before Burkett and William decided they would have to actually go to Arkansas to determine if the man was their brother. Burkett met William in Tennessee and the two traveled together to Arkansas.

During the trip William said, "It always has seemed strange to me that if brother John was alive he never communicated with Mother or Father."

"Perhaps it's just a clever trick on the part of an impostor to get part of the estate," answered Burkett. "And don't forget that all the farmland has been sold. We'll have to pay him his share in cold cash."

"An impostor would have known John and learned a lot of things about the family."

"That's so," agreed Burkett, and the two discussed questions which might help them identify this John Jones as their brother. Then Burkett said, "I know one question we can ask that only John could answer."

"What's that?"

"About the old gray mare." The brothers laughed heartily.

When the three men finally met, Burkett and William did not immediately identify the Arkansas man as their brother. All were elderly now and had changed appearance considerably since the last time they had seen one another. Burkett and William asked John scores of questions, and he answered them all correctly, but the North Carolina men could not shake the feeling that this was an impostor trying to make money from a friendship with their brother, who might be dead.

Finally William said, "Well now, John, tell us what became of the old gray mare."

John rolled back in his chair and laughed. "For heaven's sake! I'd almost forgotten all about that. When the three of us were boys, Pappy had this old gray mare. She was too old to do any work, but Pappy insisted she had to be fed and watered regularly. We three boys were tired of all the work and decided that old mare wasn't good for anything anyway, so we might as well get rid of her. We led her to a high place on the river bank and pushed her over into the stream, where she quickly drowned. We all agreed to keep that a secret as long as we lived, and this is the first time I've ever told the story!"

William looked at Burkett who was staring at him. Simultaneously they nodded their heads. "It's him!" they shouted. No doubts remained. This indeed was their brother.

N.A.

THE DAY COLD WEATHER SAVED BRYSON CITY

Thursday, Janury 27, 1910: Bryson City Court House.

Lee Francis, Registrar of Deeds for Swain County, was working late. He was not surprised to see two young local men, Onar Conley and Barrett Banks, enter his office and go directly to the steam radiators in the back of the Registrar's office. It was a cold evening, and Conley and Banks frequently came by to sit in Francis' warm office and chat. Noticing that the two men carried a familiar looking box, Francis inquired, "Is that dynamite?" The boys nodded. Francis recognized the explosive because large quantities of it had been stored throughout the court house and in nearby stores where it would remain until the spring when it would be used for road construction.

Nervously, Francis inquired, "What are you doing?"

"We are thawing it," said Conley. "It's frozen, and it won't explode unless it has been thawed." He then deposited several sticks of dynamite on the radiator.

"Well, what are you going to do with it?" asked Francis, watching the dynamite steam.

"We're going fishing," said Conley. Francis had no idea if Conley was serious or not. Onar was sort of a local Tom Sawyer with a love of practical jokes and humor. "Well, be careful. Don't blow up the court house."

Then it happened. One of the sticks fell from the radiator and struck the floor near a bundle of thawed dynamite. The explosion blew Francis from his chair. As the dynamite ignited in a series of bursts, the western end of the court house erupted. The walls, doors and windows along with the majority of records in the Registrar's office were reduced to shattered wreckage and shreds. Conley was killed instantly. Barrett lost both eyes and the majority of his teeth. Francis, suffering from multiple injuries, was not expected to live. The sound of the explosion brought residents from throughout the county to the court house where they pulled Conley, Barrett and Francis from the ruins.

An investigation on the following day verified that large quantities of dynamite in rooms adjacent to the Registrar's office had not ignited because it was frozen. In view of the fact that an equally large amount was stored in buildings near the court house, Swain County officials concluded that if the stored dynamite had not been subjected to freezing temperatures for several days prior to the accident, the village of Bryson City would have been partially destroyed.

In the coming weeks there was speculation as to what Conley and Barrett intended to do with the dynamite. Were they, indeed, going fishing? Finally, the question became irrelevant. In a letter to the Asheville *Citizen,* Mayor Picklesimer of Bryson City noted that such theorizing "...does Onar Conley, the dead boy, a positive injustice." He further noted that Conley had been a favorite among the local residents, and although the Mayor admitted Onar was high spirited, Pickelsimer felt this was often the case "with boys who become excellent citizens."

Several weeks after the incident, a friend of Banks Barrett remembered a conversation just a short time before the accident. Banks had said that his family seemed to be unlucky. "One brother lost an eye in an explosion; another lost an eye in a fight, and a third had his jaw broken." According to the *Citizen* shortly after Barrett made this statement, he lost both eyes and his teeth in the aforementioned explosion.

G.C.

168

PART V

ODDITIES AND
CURIOSITIES

THE PETRIFIED MAN

On a Friday morning in the spring of 1902, William Shipton told his hired hand, Henry, to dig a drainage ditch through the barn lot. Henry set to work at the point Shipton indicated. The digging was not difficult, and within a short time, the ditch was taking form, an ordinary ditch, until Henry's shovel met with resistance. Scraping away the dirt, he saw something that looked like a bone.

Since buried bones are common in barnyards, Henry assumed he had found the remains of a farm animal buried long ago, possibly a dog or pig. But as the earth fell away from a long appendage, the hired hand dropped his shovel and jumped out of the ditch. Yelling for his employer, Henry pointed to his discovery.

"It looks like a person's foot!" he exclaimed.

Within a short time, Shipton, with the assistance of the reluctant Henry, uncovered what appeared to be a human skeleton with a strange chalky appearance. Shipton observed that he supposed the bones were petrified and suggested they lift the skeleton from its muddy bed and carry it to the smokehouse. When the curiously rigid remains came loose from the muddy ditch with a great sucking, wet sound, Henry fled.

According to Shipton, Henry felt that the being he had unearthed was not of this world. With considerable difficulty, Shipton finally coaxed the frightened ditch digger back and managed to gain his help in carrying the "thing" to the smokehouse.

171

In short order, the excited Henry had alerted Shipton's neighbors to the discovery. By afternoon, a large number of people had gathered in front of the Shipton smokehouse to see the "petrified man." The following morning, Shipton awoke to find another crowd in his front yard. By Saturday afternoon, families were arriving from nearby communities.

Those who saw the petrified creature agreed on one significant detail. If it were indeed the remains of a man, he had borne very little resemblance to the average Homo Sapiens. According to eyewitness accounts, the creature seemed to be missing conventional parts, such as teeth, fingers and the normal number of ribs. Yet, the people stared raptly at the malformed creature for hours. Occasionally the silence would be broken by one of the observers venturing an opinion as to what "it" was.

Among the opinions quoted in the regional newspapers during the following week were theories regarding the possibility that it had been one of the "heavenly beings" cast out of Paradise. Instead of ending up in Hell with Satan, this rebel angel had fallen into what was now Shipton's barnyard.

Others suggested Henry had unearthed the remains of some missing link that had roamed the earth thousands of years ago. Others thought that maybe they were looking at the mangled remains of some poor farmer who had gone out to hunt or to find a cow over a century ago and had never returned, the victim of some freak accident.

By the following week, Shipton had decided to make the petrified thing pay for its keep. As he explained to the steady flow of visitors who continued to arrive at his farm, he had a right to "make hay while the sun shines." In effect, Shipton felt that since it had been found on his farm, it was his property. Further, he was neglecting his chores to exhibit the creature to visitors, and it seemed only right that he should have a modest recompense.

Shipton's decision to charge admission did nothing to stem the tide of visitors. Indeed, for several more months, people continued to come. Standing respectfully around the walls of the Shipton smokehouse, the spectators seemed to be lost in some sort of reverie. Some noted that the

172

grotesque creature on the floor seemed to respond to some need in the observers — a need to see tangible evidence that there are, indeed, "stranger things in heaven and earth" than Shipton's paying customers had ever dreamed of.

By the fall of 1902, the remains had become a traveling exhibit, showing up in towns throughout western North Carolina and upper South Carolina and Georgia. The "petrified bones" were also beginning to show signs of wear. In fact, the skeleton seemed to be collapsing inward.

Having received several inquiries from drummers and medicine men, Shipton decided to sell his macabre property to the highest bidder. Later — after the sale — a group of physicians inspected the bones and immediately pronounced that they were composed of plaster of Paris.

The creature was immediately dubbed the "Shipton Hoax" and a series of law suits and counter-suits were initiated.

The new owner claimed he had been tricked by Shipton; Shipton claimed that due to the legal action, his reputation had been damaged. Afterwards, many of the people who had paid money to look at the "Shipton Hoax" admitted they suspected the truth but paid their money anyway.

"I guess I just wanted to be able to say that I saw it," said one of Shipton's neighbors. "It just cost me fifteen cents to see it, and I've had a hundred dollars' worth of fun talking about it."

G.C.

NOTE: Clark Medford, the Haywood County, N.C. historian has two accounts of the "petrified man." One entitled "The Great WNC Hoax" appears in *Land O' The Sky*, and is somewhat vague in relation to geography and names. Indeed, the name Shipton is apparently fictitious, indicating that Medford wished to avoid embarrassing any surviving relatives. In *Finis and Farewell*, Medford's last book, he gives an autobiographical account of his personal encounter with the petrified man.

In the spring of 1902, Medford, a student at Cullowhee High School, traveled throughout the region during spring break selling shrubs and trees to earn his fall tuition. In this account, Medford notes that while traveling through Henderson and Transylvania counties he encountered the "petrified man." The story is essentially the same except Medford gives the name of the farmer on whose land the remains were discovered as Sittles.

G.C.

TETHERED SNAKES

During the summer of 1912, a curious story appeared in the majority of newspapers in the southern Appalachians concerning the unusual death of James Stener, "a mountaineer." In actual fact, the deceased lived in a rural area near Punxsutawney, Pennsylvania; however, the journalists of that day seemed to feel that the attending circumstances justified the descriptive phrase.

Mr. Stener was found dead near a footbridge leading to his home in the hills. Four large rattlesnakes were found on or near the dead man who had been repeatedly bitten about the face and neck.

"The man was swole up like biscuit dough," said one of the law officers who saw the body, "But the strangest thing was them snakes." According to reliable witnesses, the snakes had been tethered to the rocks near the footbridge with small leather thongs.

Stener's body was found by a party of fishermen who killed the snakes and went to the house beyond the footbridge where they talked to Stener's wife. On being told that her husband was dead, Mrs. Stener said, "Well, I guess it was bound to happen."

The fishermen learned that Stener had been putting out "guard snakes" for the past five years. "Why?" asked the bewildered fishermen.

"Well, James was terrible jealous," said the wife. She went on to explain that five years previously, Stener had taken her to a dance. When several men became overly attentive to Mrs. Stener, her husband became distressed and insisted that they return home immediately. In the days following the incident, Stener became preoccupied with the idea that men would come looking for his wife or she would go looking for them. Mrs. Stener noted that she had not left home in five years.

"Each morning, bright and early, he would go down and check on his snakes," said Mrs. Stener. Then, warning her of the consequences if she or some man should attempt to cross the footbridge, Stener would go about his chores.

"He was bad to drink and come home drunk now and then," she said. "I guess he fell down."

Several days after the tragic discovery, one of the fishermen was questioned by a journalist about the widow. How attractive was she?

"Well, she seemed a bit worse for wear," said the fisherman. "To put it another way, let's say that I was not seized by uncontrollable lust when I saw her."

G.C.

THE KING JAMES VERSION

We live in a world in which the word "wilderness" is used to designate tracts of land that are national parks or wildlife preserves. Such areas are limited and dwindling. We find it difficult to imagine a time in which America was wilderness. Vast regions of untouched forests; places where there was no path. The early settlers of the southern Appalachians found themselves in a world of gigantic trees, endless stretches of forests and thundering rivers. Sometimes large groups of settlers became lost, but because the forests teemed with wildlife and the land was fertile, there seemed little cause for concern. They cleared land, farmed and watched the seasons come and go. Gradually they forgot the old social customs and invented new ones.

In the spring of 1927, a lawyer from Richmond arrived in Waynesville, N.C. He came in response to numerous stories he had heard about the trout waters of Cataloochee and the Little Pigeon River. The lawyer was no amateur fisherman, and he arrived with enough tackle and camping gear to spend several weeks. Accustomed to living off the land, he began a trek into the deep coves of the Smoky Mountains. He found that the stories of the teeming waters were justified; each night he feasted on native brown trout.

After several days, the lawyer entered the region which the local residents called Big Bend, where the Little Pigeon swept in a great arc through a land of spectacular scenery. Here, where the river entered Tennessee, he found himself surrounded by rugged mountains and sheer cliffs that

177

dropped dramatically to the cold waters of the Pigeon. The stream-bed was littered with gigantic boulders which had been polished by wind and water until the smooth stones glowed in the sunlight like gems set in the necklace that was Big Bend. At night, he tended his tiny fire amid monoliths and listened to the respiration of the surrounding forest. The soil along the river banks contained quartz arrowheads and pottery fragments. He saw bear spoor and flushed turkey and grouse; deer watched him from the far bank. He felt himself privileged. Surely, he was in a country as yet untouched by white men.

One morning, the lawyer raised his eyes from his morning coffee to see a face staring at him from the undergrowth. The face vanished and the fisherman was left with a fragmented image. It was a child's face! To conceal his surprise the lawyer occupied himself with gathering his fishing tackle as though he intended to try his luck upstream. Leaving camp, he ventured a short distance and then returned to camp. Indeed, there was the child staring in perplexity at his fishing gear.

"Hello," said the fisherman, smiling affably at the child.

With amazing agility, the boy bolted, vanishing into the mountain fastness. The fisherman was intrigued by the occurrence. What was a lad, probably no more than nine or ten, doing here? The lawyer decided to attempt to lure the boy from hiding. He delivered a long monologue, replete with chuckles and assurances.

"No need to be afraid, lad. I mean you no harm." Picking up his fly rod, he began to cast into the Pigeon. Flicking his bait in a manner more suited to whet curiosity than to catch fish, he continued to speak. "Ever fished with a fly rod? Come on out and give it a try."

He felt, rather than saw, the boy appear. He was dressed in homespun and he was barefoot. Cautiously, he approached the man and halted some twenty yards away where he stood watching.

"Why come ye here?"

Confused by the boy's peculiar speech, the man said, "Pardon?"

"What do ye seek?"

"Why surely, lad, nothing but fish!" He picked up his creel and poured a dozen trout on the ground.

The boy regarded the fisherman soberly. Then, coming forward, he smiled tentatively.

"Watch now, I'll show you something." The man cast and the fly dropped into an eddy in the shadows of the rock cliff on the farther shore. Almost immediately, there was a strike. He laughed at the boy's open-mouthed wonder as the fish was reeled in.

"Now, you try." The lawyer offered the rod, then reconsidered and cast again. Then, he handed the boy the rod. Another strike.

"Now, reel him in. Turn the reel, there. That's right!"

And so, the boy spent an hour, alternately holding the rod and watching the man cast. To the fisherman, the boy seemed to be a normal child, filled with the delight of all children participating in a new game. The only thing unusual about him was his speech.

"Come! I would show thee something." The boy turned and walked into the woods. Perplexed, the lawyer followed. Stopping near the base of a cliff, the boy pointed to a sunken hole. Peering into the hole, the fisherman saw bones, two human skulls, a rotting boot.

"It be dangerous to come here," said the boy looking at the man with alert, solemn eyes.

"My God! Who are they?"

The boy shook his head. "I know not." Then he added, "But verily, I know who put them there."

Quickly, the lawyer retraced his steps and began to pack his gear. Within moments, he was heading for Waynesville. The boy watched him out of sight.

In Waynesville, the lawyer immediately contacted the local sheriff telling him a disconnected story about two murdered men in a pot-hole in Big Bend and the strange child who revealed their shallow grave.

"Well, this is a touchy problem," said the sheriff.

"What do you mean?"

"Big Bend is sort of an uncertain place. Nobody's quite sure where the lines run. To tell you the truth, I don't know if it's in Tennessee or North Carolina."

In the end, the sheriff contacted Tennessee and a team consisting of law enforcement officers from Haywood County, N.C. and Cocke County, TN. began the long journey down the Little Pigeon

"I think I know who we are gonna find," the sheriff told the lawyer. "Two men are missing from the Sunburst Lumber Camp here. They left to visit their families in Tennessee and never returned."

And so it was. The bodies in the shallow grave were the missing lumbermen. They had told friends that they intended to take a "short cut" home. That was months ago.

A short distance from the grave, the law officers found a settlement that no one knew existed. There were seven or eight families living on neat, well-tended farms. How long had they been there? One century? Perhaps more. The people themselves weren't sure and didn't seem to care, living with no significant contact with the 20th century world beyond the encircling mountains. There were apple orchards, wheat and corn. There were sturdy houses, cattle, barns and a sense of plenty. No, time didn't mean much in Big Bend.

Eight miles away, at Cold Springs, N.C., a storekeeper told the law officers about a young man who emerged from the woods occasionally, leading a horse loaded with butter, eggs, herbs, roots, brandy, cider and "white." He would barter for salt, matches and nails; then, vanish again into the dark forests that encircled Big Bend.

In the settlement, the officers quickly solved their murder mystery. Two men had been operating a still near the river. Mistaking the two Tennessee lumbermen for federal agents, they had murdered them. Ironically, the same child who visited the lawyer in his camp identified the murderers. As he had told the fishermen, he didn't know who the dead men were, but he "knew who put them there." The two were tried and found guilty; one was sentenced to die and, according to one story, the other spent the remainder of his life in prison.

With time, the quaint residents of Big Bend caught up with the 20th century. The homespun clothes vanished and the rigid precepts of a self-sufficient community gave way to store bought items. Eventually, the children were transported to schools where city-bred teachers stared in wonder at their crabbed, archaic handwriting. Gradually, conventional grammar replaced their outmoded speech — a speech that owed its origin to the fact that the matrons invested with the responsibility of teaching English to the children of Big Bend had relied solely on one notable textbook — the King James Version of the Bible.

G.C./N.A.

MYSTERIOUS BALDS

It is a curious fact that certain mountain tops in western North Carolina do not grow trees. These timberless peaks are easily seen and early on were labeled "bald" mountains. Why they exist is a mystery.

The altitude, or timberline, is not the reason for bald peaks since both Mount Mitchell and Clingman's Dome, each almost seven-thousand feet above sea level, grow tall trees right up to the top.

Several well-known balds — Craggy Bald, Big Bald, Hoopers Bald, Andrews Bald, Wayah Bald, Rumbling Bald, Parsons Bald, Cheoah Bald, Heintooga Bald, to name a few — are scattered throughout the region. Some appear right in the midst of or near heavy spruce or hardwood forests.

Early settlers sometimes called balds "hells" or "wooly-heads" or "slicks" because from a distance the dense growth of grasses or shrubs on the bald appears to be smooth. Travelers were often lured to what appeared to be an easy path across the mountain only to discover that the growth on a bald, which is for some reason fairly uniform, was too thick to navigate.

Explanations for the mysterious balds are many, but few have lasted. In 1938, W.A. Gates of Louisiana State University found twig gall wasps laying eggs in oak trees near summits. The infestation eventually killed the trees, so Gates concluded wasps were the reason certain areas do not have trees. The explanation does not explain why a bare spot does not get larger over the years as it should if caused by insects.

A botanist at North Carolina State College, Dr. W.B. Wells, theorized that balds were favorite campsites for Cherokees since they provided panoramic views of anyone approaching. Wells suggested that the Indians continually burned off the land for villages. To support his theory he pointed out that balds are usually gently sloping tops of mountains, not steep or rugged, and most are on the southern, protected side of the slope with nearby water — all conditions necessary for a settlement to survive. If Wells' theory is correct, then why haven't balds experienced the normal growth succession seen after fires? Why haven't pines appeared to be followed by deciduous trees?

Cherokee legend provides another explanation. One day a beast with large wings and beady eyes suddenly appeared in the sky above Nikwasi, an Indian town on the banks of the Little Tennessee River (near present day Franklin, N.C.). The horrible beast circled and then swooped down to pluck up a child and fly away. The beast returned often to steal other children, and the raids were so terrifying that the Indians took defensive action. They cleared off surrounding mountain tops and watched day and night for the beast's return.

Cherokee men searched the region looking for the beast's den, but when it was finally discovered, the den was so well fortified on a southern slope that not even the best hunter of the town could enter. So the Cherokees turned to their Great Spirit and asked for help, which they received.

The Great Spirit sent thunder and lightning down upon the beast's lair and the resulting fire killed the monster. Ever since that day, the mountain top has been a treeless bald.

At a nearby mountain top, a Cherokee sentinel who was supposed to be watching for the raiding beast, left his post. When the devastating lightning flashed through the sky and the Cherokee was not at his assigned place, he was instantly turned to stone. Today the dismal stone sentinel pays the ultimate price for lack of attention as he eternally watches from a place called Standing Indian.

While the search continues for an explanation of the balds, some of the balds have become famous. Craggy Gardens, near Asheville, N.C., may be the most well-known. When the shrubs at this bald bloom each June, tourists flock to see the colorful display. On the bald at Mount Sterling, sedges predominate, while other balds are natural homes for wildflowers, wild azaleas, rhododendron and mountain laurel.

Perhaps the strangest part of the mysterious balds story is that these unique places are rarely discussed today. How or why they exist is not written about much. Instead, balds have become favorite lookouts for sightseers. It's on a bald, among lovely blooms or gentle grasses, that tourists find unobstructed vistas and the most spectacular mountain views. For most people, the absence of trees is not even questioned, just accepted as a blessing provided by whatever Great Spirit takes care of tourists.

N.A.

THE NIGHT
THEY BURIED TRAVELER

Gary Carden was ten years old in 1945, when this "Sidney Lanier Day" at school impressed itself upon his memory.

We were herded into the auditorium of the Sylva Elementary School, a building that had been repeatedly condemned as structurally unsound. It was spring and a sharp wind was whistling outside. We sat listening to the building shift as the remainder of the elementary school filed in behind us.

"Listen," said Charlie K., my best friend that year, "I think it is going to fall down." Charlie liked to scare me. The building groaned, and we all peered raptly at the ceiling. URRRRRR. URRRRRRRRRRR. It sounded like rending timbers and ruptured steel, but we had gotten used to it.

Then, the little man came down the aisle. He was supported by two women who might have been nurses and they progressed slowly. Behind them came the principal and the mayor and a group of well-dressed folks that were probably important. But I couldn't take my eyes off the little man. He had a huge, drooping mustache and bright, blue eyes. He stared at us as he passed, stared as if we were the most exciting creatures he had ever seen.

It took them a while to get him on the stage. He was seated very near the footlights where he sat smiling and nodding down at us. The auditorium grew quiet watching the little man. Then, the principal stood at the podium and told us that our special guest for Sidney Lanier Day was Robert Lee Madison, the founder of Western Carolina Teachers College. We were told that he was a very smart man who taught, wrote poems and played music. Throughout the principal's speech the little man continued to smile and nod, his blue eyes shifting from face to face.

Mrs. Tompkins, our third grade teacher, sang "The Song of the Chattahoochee." We giggled when she acted as though she were the river: *I rush amain/to reach the plain/Split at the rock/ and together again!* Then, we all stood and quoted (shouted) "In Flanders Field." *IN FLANDERS FIELD THE POPPIES GROW/ BENEATH THE CROSSES ROW ON ROW/THAT MARK OUT PLACES.* The principal told us that "In Flanders Field" was the greatest poem that had ever been written. He read something about an eagle that was forgotten, and we stood and pledged allegiance to both the Confederate and American flags that hung on the back wall. Then, the little man talked to us.

At first we couldn't hear him, for he spoke in a hoarse whisper. He had walked to the edge of the stage, which worried the nurses, and he peered down at us like God's grandfather.

"Children, listen! I want to tell you something, and you must never forget it!" Charlie K. and I leaned forward like hooked fish. "This is a story that you must tell your children and your grandchildren. Will you do that?" Dutifully, we all nodded, our mouths open like baby birds.

"When I was a little boy like you," and he pointed right at Charlie K. and me! "I lived in Robert E. Lee's home. Yes, I did! The great leader of the Confederate army! You see, my father was a doctor and he took care of General Lee. And I used to sit in General Lee's lap when I was small like you," and he pointed at a boy in the first grade section, "and he would let me listen to his watch!" He pretended to listen to a pocket watch. "I am named for him, you know.

"But that is not important. What is important is something that I saw when I was ten. It was late at night and two of my playmates came to my bed and woke me. They said, 'Get up, Bobby!' When I asked why, they shushed me." The little man put his finger to his lips. "Shhhhhh, and I got up and followed them. We hid in the ditch by the barn. The moon was out and my friends pointed to the road that ran from the barn. "They will come from there," said one of my friends. "Watch and be quiet."

"Then I heard it!" The little man was excited now, and he leaned down toward our upturned faces.

"Theratt! tat! tat! tat! It was the sound of drums." He pretended to be beating a drum.

"Theratt! tat! tat! tat! And the great barn doors swung open.

"Hidden there in the ditch, we saw the drummers, and behind them, the torches. Oh, it was bright as day, children. And then came General Lee. He walking with his hat in his hand, and he was in full uniform. Behind him came the wagon.

"It was one of the old ammunition wagons from the War, and it was draped in gray ... gray like General Lee's uniform.

"'What is it?' I said, 'What is in the wagon?'

"'It's Traveler,' they said, 'General Lee's horse. Traveler's dead.'

"It was a military funeral, same as would be given any soldier that died in General Lee's army. So, we stood, my playmates and I, and we watched them pass. On down the road, into the fog.

"Oh, lots of things have happened to this old man, children. I've seen life at its cruelest, and when it approached the sublime. Heard music, seen sunsets and tasted wine. But the image that I will carry to my grave is seeing those torches flare in the night, and hearing the drums: THERATT! TAT! TAT! TAT! And seeing General Lee walk by with his hat in his hand. And that wagon passing, that wagon draped in gray."

For a moment, the little man seemed to have forgotten us. Then, he laughed and said, "Remember that, children. When you are old like me, tell your grandchildren. Tell them about this old man who was there the night they buried Traveler."

The little man's eyes sparkled with tears that ran down that great walrus mustache. "Oh, the stories that I could tell you! Sad, wonderful and magic."

The nurses came forward and grasped the little man's arms and led him from the stage. We sat silently watching the nurses lead Dr. Robert L. Madison up the aisle.

Several years ago, I had occasion to tell this story to a group of teachers at the North Carolina Center for the Advancement of Teaching at Cullowhee, N.C. The story seemed appropriate since the subject of the conference was myth and legend, and here we were close to the college that Madison had founded. The group's facilitator noted that the story could not possibly be true since Traveler's skeleton had been exhibited at Washington and Lee for years. He looked at me knowingly. "I know how you storytellers fabricate," he said. "This is one of your folktales, isn't it?" I assured him it was true.

The facilitator smiled. "Well, let's move along now."

I was troubled by the incident. Had I fabricated it? I'd had fifty years to shape and reshape Dr. Madison's visit. How much had I created? While doing research for this book, I talked to Richard Wilson of Sylva, the great-great grandson of Dick Wilson, the murdered man in "The Hanging of Jack Lambert." We talked about how memory distorted the past. Then, I happened to mention my misgivings about Dr. Madison's story about Traveler.

Richard Wilson said, "You mean, the story of how he hid in the ditch and watched the wagon ... and the torches ... and heard the drums beating?" I was stunned.

"Yes," I said, "How did you know that?"

"I was in the second grade," said Richard Wilson. "I was sitting behind you."

I am most pleased to have Richard Wilson validate my memory. But perhaps the truth in this instance is ... academic. Even without factual data, the story is true because it exists in my memory (and in Richard Wilson's).

I believed Robert Lee Madison when I was ten, and I believe him now. I see those children huddled in a weed-grown ditch, their awed faces washed by torchlight. And the drums. I hear the drums, and I can see the sad, gray man walking with his hat in his hand. Dr. Madison asked me to tell you, and I have kept my promise.

G.C.

TO PAY THE NATIONAL DEBT

In 1938, a resident of Brevard, N.C. found a collection of old newspapers in the attic. Among them was an issue of *The Sylvan Valley News* which was dated 1902 and claimed to be "the only paper published in Transylvania County." Among the news stories was one entitled "Hugging Social Success." According to the article, one of the community churches which had incurred a substantial debt decided to initiate a new and somewhat radical fund-raising effort. The church advertised a "hugging social." Specifically, the female members of the congregation agreed to participate in some serious hugging under the following conditions and limitations:

Two-minute hugs .... 15 cents

15 to 25 minute hugs .... 50 cents

(If someone else's wife) .... $1 additional charge

(Old Maids) .... .03 cents and no time limit.

According to the editor of the *Sylvan Valley News,* the church had substantially reduced its debt. More than six-hundred people had attended the hugging social, and plans were underway to hold another which would, hopefully, erase the debt. The editor further noted that the ladies were to be commended for their humor and good will; he asked that the church inform him of the date of the next event as he planned to be present with his .03 cents.

G.C.

THE SMOKE OF THE GODS

In an isolated cove in what is now called the Canada Community of Jackson County, N.C., the smoke from the ancient townhouse of the Cherokee gods still rises toward the heavens. A colorless, warm vapor, the smoke, the Cherokees believed, was produced by the fire of the Nunnehi, "The Immortals." To any visitor who kneels before the chasm, there is little to suggest he might be standing on the boundary between our world and another where time and space are meaningless. Small stones dropped into the opening rattle and click, cascading downwards ... faint echoes, and then silence.

According to Cherokee mythology, the Nunnehi were indifferent to the laws governing mortals. They could live where they wished: in the heavens, at the bottom of lakes or under the earth. There they pursued a daily life very much like ours — hunting, fishing and dancing. The Nunnehi dearly loved to dance, and since they never felt hunger, sickness or old age, they danced a great deal. Life was good for the Nunnehi. They had appetites, but they were not enslaved by them. They ate and drank, but for pleasure only ...never for need. Their deer grazed on the bottoms of lakes, and their fish swam in cloud-shrouded rivers in the heavens. It is of little wonder, then, that the smoke from their underground townhouses should not only be clear but thought to have supernatural powers.

There is a story of a Cherokee youth named Rone who lived before the white man came. He fell in love with the Chief's daughter, and she with him. But the Chief found Rone an undesirable son-in-law. Too young, too callow, too poor. Hoping that his daughter might find favor with a man of wealth and power, the Chief sent Rone on a long journey, a tedious errand that would take almost a year to complete. "Out of sight, out of mind," thought the Chief. "My daughter will forget him. Before he returns from the ocean-bound edge of the world, she will be a young wife with a child."

The Chief was wrong. His daughter was stricken with melancholy. She no longer took pleasure in food, friends or the face of her father. Each evening she sat, looking down the trail on which Rone had departed. She grew sick, and her father found he could not rouse her. Before long, she no longer stirred from her bed, and the Chief realized her only hope for survival lay in Rone's return.

When Rone finally returned, the daughter was barely alive. When Rone spoke to her, she did not respond, for she had withdrawn within. Already, the medicine man had begun the death chant when Rone picked her up, the frail shadow of his love. Striding from the Chief's lodge, he climbed the mountain, hurrying through the dark woods until he came to the place where the warm air rushed upwards. Working rapidly, he built a woven bed of saplings which he hung between two trees on either side of the chasm. He placed the pale, young girl in the rustic litter, suspended between this world and the other. The warm air flowed over her. She slept and Rone tended her all that night and the next. When she recognized his face and smiled, he knew she would live. She had been healed by Nunnehi smoke rising from a world where death and sickness have no power.

Some of the old ones in the Canada Community know the story of Rone, passed down from "a grandfather's grandfather." They also say they remember visiting the smoke hole in the dead of winter. The warm air would melt the snow for a radius of five feet around the chasm. Hunters would kneel there to warm their hands and to inhale the rising vapor. "Warms the body and the soul," the hunters used to say, and they returned to the woods refreshed and renewed.

No one visits the smoke hole now. Times have changed, bringing new roads. The waters of an artificial lake surround the rocky ledge above the chasm. People who know its exact location are rare. "Somewhere over there, I think," old-timers say. "I'm not right sure, to tell the truth. Easy to find in winter, though. Then you can see that warm air rising in fog; see that bare circle of earth in the snow."

When I asked about the smoke hole in a little grocery store in Tuckaseegee, receiving vague directions, an old man by the stove raised his head and smiled. "That place will cure your rheumatism," he said. "Cured mine, and that's the truth."

N.A./G.C.

Shuler family at base of giant tree in 1930s.
This family did not live in the tree.

BIG TREES AND THEIR INHABITANTS

The first trappers, hunters, traders and renegades who entered the southern Appalachians found dense virgin forests full of huge poplar, chestnut and oak trees. It may be difficult to imagine today, but those untouched trees were not just big, they often were gigantic. Many had trunks twenty feet or more across, and they were important to human survival. Some, like the Qualla Reservation Boundary Tree, became famous. Others were landmarks used to direct travelers, and always the big trees provided more than shade. Some became home to men as well as squirrels.

Scores of mountain stories tell of people who found shelter in the decayed base of a big tree or of people who setup housekeeping in a tree. The only photographs of these massive trees are from a later era when logging companies began harvesting mountain timber. In some of the photographs we see whole families at the base of a gigantic poplar or chestnut, and it is obvious that the tree was as wide across as many of today's dwellings. A man could live quite comfortably in one of these big trees, and many did.

Near where the Georgia and North Carolina state lines meet there was once an herb doctor who lived a focused, harmonious life in the hollow of a large chestnut tree. He gathered native herbs which he both used and sold to pharmaceutical companies while residing in his tree house.

Near Cashiers, N.C., is Stumphouse Mountain, and the source of the mountain's name has been variously explained. One tale insists a Cherokee woman lived in one of the mountain's large trees. Another story says that a roof was constructed across several high-standing tree stumps, and living residents will point to one or more existing stumps and say, "Now that's where they used to hide their white lightning."

By the turn of the 20th century, some of the truly big trees had earned names. The Fed Poplar in Macon County, N.C. is one people still talk about. Furman Raby feels sure he, like the other Rabys of western North Carolina, descended from one Frederick Raby, the poplar tree's famous inhabitant. No genealogist has been able to support the idea, but then family memories of "what the old people said" varies on other things, too. Whatever the details, the fact remains that one huge poplar tree was named "the Fed Poplar" after Frederick Raby.

Unlucky enough to be at a Polk County dance the night a fight broke out, young Frederick Raby was there when a rock was thrown and a man died. Raby was convicted of the crime, but he was not sentenced to death. Instead, he was branded with a large "M" on his forehead and smaller letters in the palms of his hands. Then he was set free. While his life had been spared, as a branded man, Raby was not safe. The M's on his body announced an open season on Frederick; he could be shot by anyone and there would be no retribution.

Raby headed for the dense forests and started walking west, away from Polk County. He crossed the high Balsams, finally stopping at a broad valley, now called Cowee Valley, in Macon County. There, on Bee Branch, Frederick Raby found an ancient poplar tree which was strong and healthy but also hollow in the lower part of the trunk. Inside the tree he constructed a crude sleeping loft and built a ladder. Once he climbed into his tree house and brought the ladder up behind him, he was safe and unseen.

As Frederick carefully began to explore his neighborhood, the marked man developed a path across the ridge, through Denton Cove and into the next valley. Older residents can still point to the "Fed Trail" and will gladly explain that they were told Fed had a still in the neighboring cove which he checked on regularly.

"Ah, yes, the Fed Trail. Aunt Laura Dalton used to talk about it every time she'd come to visit, " said seventy-nine-year-old Grace Shuler Raby. "She'd tell the same story, and we loved hearing it. Uncle Fed's Trail. Aunt Laura Dalton would tell us over and over again how he killed people he met on the trail and buried them under leaves. She'd sometimes point out a log and say Fed hid a body behind it." Grace never tired of Aunt Laura's stories. "Why we'd see her coming, and she'd be standing in the road all by herself, pointing to the mountains, tracing out the old Fed Trail. That Aunt Laura was something."

Whether Fed was as fierce as Aunt Laura's tales is doubtful, for apparently Frederick married. When a young Cope girl, whose family lived at the head of the creek, happened upon him, she wasn't frightened. She didn't see a branded renegade but a hungry fellow, not that much older than she was. She began to secretly bring him food, and it has been assumed the two married, exactly when is unknown. There may have been a second wife, too, because family historians have found evidence that Frederick was married to a young woman from Tennessee. Whether it took one or two wives, Frederick fathered almost a dozen children, and some of their descendants remain in Cowee Valley.

At some point Frederick left his poplar home and lived in a conventional cabin, but the tree remained a useful landmark. Grace Raby remembers taking shelter from rainstorms in the tree, and more than one living resident describes the tree's size with "You could turn a ten-foot fence rail around inside the tree." Grace Raby said, "Why it was lots bigger than my bathroom now."

In the 1940s the tree was cut, and some of the men who used nine-foot cross cut saws to fell the tree are still alive. One of the lumbermen recalls hearing that Fed Raby lived in the tree to hide out the Civil War, and whether that was true or not is also debatable. What is true is that felling the Fed Poplar was a full day's work, and the trunk had to be quartered before it could be loaded onto trucks. It was sold to a man in Murphy, N.C., and no one knows exactly what the lumber was used for, but the stump remains. And so do the stories of the big tree.

About three mountains away is another big tree legend, one slightly younger than the Fed Poplar but one that provides more evidence of the size of mountain timber. At the head of Barker's Creek is a cabin built entirely from the lumber of one tree. Older residents such as Gardner Gunther are quick to say, "Now it ain't the oldest cabin," an addition to the facts which isn't true, they say. "Old Stanberry Jones built the cabin with his father, Lyle," said Gunther. "When I was a young man, living next to old Stance, he would light that big crooked pipe of his, put in the tobacco he either grew himself or ordered from Kentucky and tell about building the cabin. He was an old man, then, but his dad had bought the land higher up because timber was where your paycheck was in those days. When Stanberry found this big tree, he knew there was a lot of lumber there, and he built that cabin entirely by hand and entirely from that one yellow poplar."

The cabin later became a bit of a tourist attraction in the late '40s and '50s after it was bought by a couple who advertised it as the oldest cabin in the area. Another cabin was added to the original structure making a two-cabin house with a dog trot. Photographs of the cabin hung in local restaurants and newspaper stories were written about how one tree had provided enough lumber for the dwelling.

Although the cabin has been modified by each successive owner, it has been lucky in that none of the occupants have covered up or destroyed the original carefully notched and fitted hand-hewn timbers. The current owner has landscaped around the cabin and kept the nearby shed and a barn in good condition. Even with the addition of a modern kitchen and thousands of dollars in landscaping, the original cabin's exterior remains awe-inspiring. From one tree mere humans cut and planed planks as wide as three feet and fit them together into a structure which still stands and which continues to evoke admiration.

N.A.

Cabin made from one tree. Notice the size of the timbers in relation to the furniture.

BE CAREFUL WHAT YOU WISH FOR...

A 1911 issue of the Waynesville *Courier* carries a news story concerning the death of one "Tom Mashburn, an escaped convict from a chain gang in Georgia." Mashburn had been arrested by Will Hyde, Deputy Sheriff from Robbinsville, N.C. As Hyde and two assistants were transporting Mashburn to jail, the prisoner began to lament his bad luck, saying he "had rather die than go back to the chain gang." Hyde, who had been drinking heavily, consulted his assistants, and the three men agreed that Mashburn would probably be better off dead. "While the other two held Mashburn, Hyde shot him through the heart. The three men were committed to jail, having given themselves up."

G.C.

A WONDROUS SNAKE

(The following letter was published in the North Carolina Citizen, circa August 1, 1872.)

Several weeks ago while Sylvester Bowman of Clairborne County was cutting the sprouts off his oats, he saw what he took to be a large black snake and struck at it with his scythe, when to his astonishment, the snake struck at him with its tail, lifting its tail several feet from the earth. Bowman, whereupon again struck at the snake, but the vicious reptile, not at all intimidated, returned the blow and pressed Bowman so closely that it was with difficulty he got away. Returning to the attack, Bowman by means of large rocks, at last succeeded in crippling the snake and fastened it to the earth. With the assistance of Jordan F. Longmire, it was now examined and to their astonishment was found to be six feet long and to have a horn at the end of its tail a little over an inch and a quarter long, shaped like a rooster's Spur. (sic) But what was more astonishing, it had two eyes in its tail, which, excepting the horn, was shaped exactly like the head but not so large. Indeed, to see the tail, one would have thought that it was the head and the horn was its tongue. The horn was very sharp. The snake seemed very fierce at its tail end, and endeavored to strike everything that came near its tail. Various experiments were performed to ascertain whether it could see with the eye in its tail, and it was demonstrated beyond doubt that it could see with its tail eyes. These eyes had lids which opened and shut and gleamed with anger.

Indeed, the tail head seemed far more fierce than the other head. Although the snake tapered somewhat from its main head, still the tail head was as thick as a large thumb and as blunt.

Mr. Bowman carried the snake home while disabled, but it continued to strike at every intruder with its horn, and the family became alarmed. Mr. Bowman shot it dead.

Messrs. Bowman and Longmire vouch for the truthfulness of these statements and so will many other citizens of the neighborhood. The writer of this knows Mr. Longmire to be a truthful man, a man of wealth and intelligence and an old member of the Methodist Church.

Jacksonboro, Tenn., July 21, 1872

G.C.

3 4200 00502 5792

NEW HANOVER COUNTY PUBLIC LIBRARY
201 Chestnut Street
Wilmington, N.C. 28401

GAYLORD S